"No volume for the armchair dreamer who longs for results, this author's collection is a spirited manual for action, for risk taking and courageous leaps. It is a call to march with intuition and clarity toward solution and truth. Roll up your sleeves when you tackle this 'tiger'; you are headed for adventure that will inspire any who dare to follow."

—MARK O. HATFIELD, U.S. senator, retired

"Our world is under constant challenging pressures that create both promise and peril possibilities. The future will most likely be determined by the leadership of our nations and institutions that form our society. The key is being able to deal with the diversity of issues and peoples with a solid perspective of faith, integrity and vision. This book is a wonderful compilation of quotations that provides perspectives of our leaders."

—R.J. INGERSOLL, corporate vice president,
The Boeing Company

"Gordon Jackson's volume, *Never Scratch a Tiger with a Short Stick,* demonstrates his insight on critical issues of leadership. His chosen quotes demonstrate his grasp of the challenges faced by leaders as people in challenging circumstances with multiple constituencies. His quotes on change will be particularly useful to those facing the rapidly-changing environments with today's academic or business world. This is a volume that is a useful addition to any leader's library."

—M.R.C. GREENWOOD, PH.D.
chancellor, University of California, Santa Cruz

Never

Scratch a Tiger with a Short Stick

And Other
Quotations
for Leaders

COMPILED BY
GORDON S. JACKSON

NAVPRESS®

BRINGING TRUTH TO LIFE

OUR GUARANTEE TO YOU

We believe so strongly in the message of our books that we are making this quality guarantee to you. If for any reason you are disappointed with the content of this book, return the title page to us with your name and address and we will refund to you the list price of the book. To help us serve you better, please briefly describe why you were disappointed. Mail your refund request to: NavPress, P.O. Box 35002, Colorado Springs, CO 80935.

The Navigators is an international Christian organization. Our mission is to reach, disciple, and equip people to know Christ and to make Him known through successive generations. We envision multitudes of diverse people in the United States and every other nation who have a passionate love for Christ, live a lifestyle of sharing Christ's love, and multiply spiritual laborers among those without Christ.

NavPress is the publishing ministry of The Navigators. NavPress publications help believers learn biblical truth and apply what they learn to their lives and ministries. Our mission is to stimulate spiritual formation among our readers.

www.navpress.com

ISBN 1-57683-342-9

NAVPRESS, BRINGING TRUTH TO LIFE, and the NAVPRESS logo are registered trademarks of NavPress. Absence of ® in connection with marks of NavPress or other parties does not indicate an absence of registration of those marks.

Cover design by David Carlson
Photo by PhotoDisc
Creative Team: Don Simpson, Kathy Rue, Glynese Northam

Unless otherwise identified, all Scripture quotations in this publication are taken from the HOLY BIBLE: NEW INTERNATIONAL VERSION® (NIV®). Copyright © 1973, 1978, 1984 by International Bible Society. Used by permission of Zondervan Publishing House. All rights reserved.

Never scratch a tiger with a short stick and other quotations for
leaders / compiled by Gordon S. Jackson.
    p. cm.
Includes bibliographical references and index.
  ISBN 1-57683-342-9
  1. Leadership--Quotations, maxims, etc. I. Jackson, Gordon, 1949-
  BF637.L4N48 2003
  158'.4--dc21   2003002395

Printed in the United States of America

3 4 5 6 7 8 9 10 11 12 / 10 09 08 07 06 05

FOR A FREE CATALOG OF
NAVPRESS BOOKS & BIBLE STUDIES,
CALL 1-800-366-7788 (USA)
OR 1-800-839-4769 (CANADA)

To the memory of Howard Gage,
a good friend and one of the quiet leaders.

TOPICS BY CATEGORY

7

PART 5: LEADERSHIP AT WORK
    — ITS OUTCOMES

PART 6: THE LEADER'S CAREER

PART 7: MISCELLANEOUS

TOPICS BY CATEGORY

TOPICS IN ALPHABETICAL ORDER

TOPICS IN ALPHABETICAL ORDER

ACKNOWLEDGMENTS

Several sets of thanks are due. First, I'm grateful to Keith Beebe, Laura Bloxham, Rick Boutz, Jack Burns, Mo Copeland, Carl Green, Helen Higgs, Mark Mosrie, Greg Orwig, Frieda and Min Warshore, and Bill Zobrist for their help in introducing me to some of the quotations included in this collection or for reading various drafts of the manuscript.

Next, I am indebted to the many writers on leadership, both scholarly and popular, from whose work I have drawn directly and to those scores of anthologists whose efforts have provided much additional material.

Finally, thanks also are due to Martha Brown for her consistently fine secretarial help, and to my wife, Sue, and daughter, Sarah, who helped with the less-than-scintillating task of manuscript preparation.

INTRODUCTION

Whether they welcome the task or not, leaders are continually called upon to scratch the tigers in the organizations they serve. They must do so not knowing exactly where the tiger is itching, how long a stick to use, or just how hard to scratch. Scratching too softly won't satisfy the tiger, and scratching too hard could introduce a host of new problems. All the leader knows is that the tiger is there, he's itchy, and the leader is the one to whom it falls to carry out this high-stakes task. He or she must do so with courage and skill, relying on incomplete information, and in full view of a captivated audience, not all of whom necessarily want a contented tiger.

This notion of scratching a tiger, and finding the right-sized stick to do so, encapsulates some key aspects of a leader's duties. For every leader has three basic concerns: the task at hand, the tools to do it, and the wisdom to know how to proceed. But as with any metaphor, this one too can be carried beyond its usefulness; its purpose here is simply to indicate that this commonsense advice exemplifies well the purpose of this anthology. And that is to offer leaders useful reminders of principles they already know, as well as fresh ideas to equip them for their roles and enable them to think in new ways about the nature, demands, and rewards of leadership.

The quotes included here derive from two assumptions. The first is that in addition to its highly public nature, leadership has a core of qualities that is common to leaders throughout society. Thus, whether you're a CEO of a Fortune 500 corporation or a mid-level manager, a school principal, a member of Congress, a pastor or rabbi, a military officer, or a director of an inner-city food bank, as a leader you have taken on a particular set of explicit and implicit responsibilities. All leaders, regardless of their sphere of operation, need to be concerned with who's following them and why, what kind of leadership they are providing, where they intend to go, and how they intend to get there. This anthology is designed to help you think through your commitments in each of those areas.

In addition to assuming that leaders have core qualities in common, this book also assumes that leaders never stop learning to lead. Like doctors, lawyers, and teachers, for example, leaders constantly need to expand their knowledge and perspectives and be reminded of what they already know. Warren Bennis and Burt Nanus say that learning leadership is like learning to play the violin in public. The quotes selected here are therefore designed to help anyone who's learning that instrument. Whether beginners, fairly adept, or playing at concert hall levels, leaders share several characteristics. Not the least of which is their common need for the encouragement, inspiration, reminders of basics, warnings or sound advice that this volume is designed to provide.

To provide an eclectic set of insights on these key dimensions of leadership, I've tried to select quotes whose familiarity indicates they've already proven their lasting value, as well as lesser known contributions that can offer you new ideas and perspectives. The quotations are divided into seventy topics, which are arranged by alphabetical order and are cross-referenced to each other. An additional list of contents is provided on page 7, in which the topics are clustered into seven sections. This listing will be useful if you're seeking quotations that deal with a more focused area, such as "The Nature of Leadership," for example, or "The Leader's Career." You can also search for quotations by author, using the author index at the end of the book.

This anthology is indebted to numerous leadership books and a wide range of other written materials, including other collections of quotations. Quotes from these sources have augmented my own collection of quotations that I have compiled over the past several decades. While I have striven for as high a level of accuracy as possible in recording the hundreds of voices represented here, it is inevitable that some errors, misquotations, or incorrect attributions will be included. Tracking down the precise and original wording of a quote is sometimes a slippery task, as is determining who in fact said or wrote a quote attributed to several speakers or writers. Where necessary, I've tried to find the most reliable and authoritative versions of the quotations I've included. On occasion, I've provided brief descriptions of the speaker or the context of the quote where I thought that would enrich your understanding.

Despite my attempts to present a breadth of perspectives in this collection, relatively few quotations come from non-western sources. The reason that American and British sources dominate is not because these writers and speakers have a monopoly on thinking about leadership. Regrettably, written quotes from non-western sources are comparatively scarce. Similarly, most of the quotes are from men, reflecting the reality that male voices have typically dominated leadership roles in virtually all sectors of our society. Also, some quotations refer to "man," "men," "mankind," or similar generic references to people. As products of an earlier era, these quotations lack the inclusive language that increasingly marks contemporary English. In keeping with a concern to record all quotations accurately, these were included unchanged.

Some of the material that follows draws in part from the prodigious amount of scholarly and popular literature on leadership that has appeared in the past two decades, as this concept has received increasing attention in contemporary western society. Yet this anthology is not intended to provide a systematic overview of this rich body of material. What follows is purely a personal selection of quotes that I believe will appeal to people in leadership positions. Nor does this volume seek to reflect or advance any one of the several schools of thought currently marking our understanding of leadership. If this book has a bias, it would be toward the notion of servant leadership, a concept popularized by Robert Greenleaf. And if it has a bias against any material, it would be to exclude or minimize the cynicism toward leadership that tends to mark much popular culture in the contemporary United States. Far from seeing managers and leaders with the cynical or even nihilistic views of cartoon characters like "Dilbert" or "The Simpsons," this volume unapologetically regards good leadership as something to be encouraged and nurtured at all levels and in all sectors of our society. Leaders we will always have with us; our task is to seek out, nurture, and hold accountable the best ones we can. It is my hope that this book can in some modest way help to attain that end.

ACTION

The greatest pleasure in life is doing what people say you cannot do. —Walter Bagehot

Action springs not from thought, but from a readiness for responsibility. —Dietrich Bonhoeffer

Nothing is more terrible than activity without insight. —Thomas Carlyle

Talk doesn't cook rice. —Chinese proverb

Deliberation is a function of the many; action is the function of one. —Charles de Gaulle

O Lord God, when Thou givest to thy servants to endeavour any great matter, grant us also to know that it is not the beginning, but the continuing of the same until it is thoroughly finished, which yieldeth the true glory. —Sir Francis Drake

Hell, there are no rules here—we're trying to accomplish something. —Thomas Edison

First say to yourself what you would be; and then do what you have to do. —Epictetus

If you think you can do a thing or think you can't do a thing, you're right. —Henry Ford

You have a zero percent scoring average on shots you don't take. —Wayne Gretzky

Never confuse motion with action.

—ERNEST HEMINGWAY

To dispose a soul to action we must upset its equilibrium.

— ERIC HOFFER

Deliberate with caution, but act with decision; and yield with graciousness or oppose with firmness.   —CHARLES HOLE

The biggest sin is sitting on your ass.

—FLORYNCE KENNEDY

It is motive alone that gives character to the actions of men.

—JEAN DE LA BRUYÈRE

I have always thought the actions of men the best interpreters of their thoughts.   —JOHN LOCKE

Trust no Future, howe'er pleasant! Let the dead Past bury its dead! Act—act in the living Present!

—HENRY WADSWORTH LONGFELLOW

Existence was given us for action. Our worth is determined by the good deeds we do, rather than by the fine emotions we feel.   —E. L. MAGOON

There comes a moment when you have to stop revving up the car and shove it into gear.   —DAVID MAHONEY

You don't think much of my methods. I don't either. But I like my way of doing it better than your way of not doing it.

—DWIGHT L. MOODY

Action, to be effective, must be directed to clearly conceived ends.
                                                            —JAWAHARLAL NEHRU

Don't tell me it can't be done until you have spent at least four hours trying.
                                                            —BOB PIERCE

The whole point about getting things done is knowing what to leave undone.
                                                            —LADY READING

Pray to God but keep rowing toward the shore.
                                                            —RUSSIAN PROVERB

Heaven never helps the man who will not act.
                                                            —SOPHOCLES

It is not the same to talk of bulls as to be in the bull ring.
                                                            —SPANISH PROVERB

To understand is hard. Once one understands, action is easy.
                                                            —SUN YAT SEN

If thou has commenced a good action, leave it not incomplete.
                                                            —THE TALMUD

We should be taught not to wait for inspiration to start a thing. Action always generates inspiration. Inspiration seldom generates action.
                                                            —FRANK TIBOLT

Life does not consist in thinking, it consists in acting.
                                                            —WOODROW WILSON

See also Change; Effort and Work; Initiative; Results

ADVICE

If you really want to give me advice, do it on Saturday afternoon between one and four o'clock, when you've got twenty-five seconds to do it, between plays. Don't give me advice on Monday. I know the right thing to do on Monday.

—ALEX AGASE, FOOTBALL COACH

There are few if any ways to determine previously the rightness or wrongness of certain courses of action. There is, however, a helpful principle. He who seeks the advice and counsel of others will be more right than if he did not.

—LAWRENCE APPLEY

Advice is judged by results, not by intentions.

—CICERO

Never give advice unless asked.

—GERMAN PROVERB

To accept good advice is but to increase one's own ability.

— JOHANN WOLFGANG VON GOETHE

Advice is less necessary to the wise than to fools, but the wise derive most advantage from it. —FRANCESCO GUICCIARDINI

Whatever advice you give, be short.

—HORACE

He is bad that will not take advice, but he is a thousand times worse who takes every advice. —IRISH PROVERB

Advice is what we ask for when we already know the answer but wish we didn't. —ERICA JONG

No man is so foolish but he may sometimes give another good counsel, and no man so wise that he may not easily err if he takes no other counsel than his own. He that is taught only by himself has a fool for a master.　　　—BEN JONSON

You will always find a few Eskimos ready to tell the Congolese how to cope with the heat.　　　—STANISLAW LEC

Good counsel has no price.

—GUISEPPE MAZZINI

Every man, however wise, needs the advice of some sagacious friend in the affairs of life.　　　—PLAUTUS

Kings stand more in need of the company of the intelligent than the intelligent do of the society of kings.　　　—SAADI

The true secret of giving advice is, after you have honestly given it, to be perfectly indifferent whether it is taken or not and never persist in trying to set people straight.

—HANNAH WHITALL SMITH

Many receive advice, few profit by it.

—PUBLILIUS SYRUS

The President cannot function without advisers or without advice, written or oral. But just as soon as he is required to show what kind of advice he has had, who said what to him, or what kind of records he has, the advice he receives will be worthless.　　　—HARRY S. TRUMAN

The President hears a hundred voices telling him that he is the greatest man in the world. He must listen carefully indeed to hear the one voice that tells him he is not.　　　—HARRY S. TRUMAN

AMBITION — PROMISE AND PITFALLS

Ambition is the subtlest Beast of the Intellectual and Moral Field. It is wonderfully adroit in concealing itself from its owner. —JOHN ADAMS

Ambition can creep as well as soar.

—EDMUND BURKE

To reach the height of our ambition is like trying to reach the rainbow; as we advance it recedes. —EDMUND BURKE

He who sacrifices his conscience to ambition burns a picture to obtain the ashes. —CHINESE PROVERB

It is by attempting to reach the top in a single leap that so much misery is caused in the world. —WILLIAM COBBETT

Ambition makes the same mistake concerning power, that avarice makes as to wealth. She begins by accumulating it as a means to happiness, and finishes by continuing to accumulate it as an end. —CHARLES CALEB COLTON

All ambitions are lawful except those which climb upward on the miseries or credulities of mankind. —JOSEPH CONRAD

Time was when I could not sleep for ambition. I thought of nothing but fame and immortality. I could not bear the idea of dying and being forgotten. —ANTHONY ASHLEY COOPER

Accurst ambition,
How dearly I have bought you.

—JOHN DRYDEN

The significance of a man is not in what he attains but rather in what he longs to attain. —KAHLIL GIBRAN

Nothing arouses ambition so much in the heart as the trumpet-clang of another's fame. —BALTASAR GRACIÁN

Ambition is not a weakness unless it be disproportioned to the capacity. To have more ambition than ability is to be at once weak and unhappy. —G. S. HILLARD

Where ambition ends happiness begins.

—HUNGARIAN PROVERB

Whenever a man has cast a longing eye on offices, a rottenness begins in his conduct. —THOMAS JEFFERSON

The slave has only one master; the ambitious man has as many as there are persons whose aid may contribute to the advancement of his fortunes. —JEAN DE LA BRUYÈRE

One often passes from love to ambition but rarely returns from ambition to love. —DUC DE LA ROCHEFOUCAULD

Ambition is so powerful a passion in the human breast, that however high we reach we are never satisfied. —MACHIAVELLI

Avarice walks among us disguised as ambition.

—EZRA J. MISHAN

Ambition is the spur that makes men struggle with destiny. It is heaven's own incentive to make purpose great and achievement greater. —DONALD G. MITCHELL

Men may be popular without being ambitious; but there is rarely an ambitious man who does not try to be popular.

—FREDERICK NORTH

I must keep aiming higher and higher—even though I know how silly it is.

—ARISTOTLE ONASSIS

Throw away all ambition beyond that of doing the day's work well.

—WILLIAM OSLER

My success so far has only been won by absolute indifference to my future career.

—THEODORE ROOSEVELT

I charge thee, fling away ambition. By that sin fell the angels; how can man then, the image of his maker, hope to win by it?

—WILLIAM SHAKESPEARE, *Henry VIII*

Ambition is an idol on whose wings great minds are carried to extremes: to be sublimely great, or to be nothing.

—THOMAS SOUTHERN

If you would be Pope, you can think of nothing else.

—SPANISH PROVERB

ANGER

We praise a man who is angry on the right grounds, against the right persons, in the right manner, at the right moment, and for the right length of time.

—ARISTOTLE

How much more grievous are the consequences of anger than the causes of it.

—MARCUS AURELIUS

In the midst of great joy, do not promise anyone anything. In the midst of great anger, do not answer anyone's letter.

—Chinese proverb

A man is as big as the things that make him angry.

—Winston Churchill

When anger rises, think of the consequences.

—Confucius

Of all bad things by which mankind are cursed
Their own bad tempers surely are the worst.

—Richard Cumberland

Anger is an expensive luxury in which only men of a certain income can indulge.

—G. W. Curtis

To rule one's anger is well; to prevent it is still better.

—Tryon Edwards

If you would cure anger, do not feed it. Say to yourself, "I used to be angry every day; then every other day; now only every third or fourth day." When you reach thirty days offer a sacrifice of thanksgiving to the gods.

—Epictetus

I have learned through bitter experience the one supreme lesson to conserve my anger, and as heat conserved is transmitted into energy, even so our anger controlled can be transmitted into a power that can move the world.

—Mahatma Gandhi

He who restrains his anger overcomes his greatest enemy.

—Latin proverb

Always remember that when you are in the right you can afford to keep your temper, and when you are in the wrong you cannot afford to lose it. —JOHN J. REYNOLDS

Anger, if not restrained, is frequently more hurtful to us than the injury that provokes it. —SENECA

The best cure for anger is delay.

—SENECA

Anger gets us into trouble. Pride keeps us there.

—UNKNOWN

Never get angry except on purpose.

—UNKNOWN JAPANESE DIPLOMAT

See also Self-Discipline

BOLDNESS

Given an equal degree of intelligence, a thousand times more is lost in war through anxiety than through boldness.

— CARL VON CLAUSEWITZ

Men of principle are always bold, but bold men are not always men of principle. —CONFUCIUS

Fortune befriends the bold.

—JOHN DRYDEN

Any coward can fight a battle when he's sure of winning; but give me the man who has pluck to fight when he's sure of losing. —George Eliot

Fortune favors the audacious.

— Erasmus

In great straits, when hope is small, the boldest counsels are the safest. —Livy

Don't stand shivering upon the bank; plunge in at once, and have it over. —Sam Slick

Only the bold get to the top.

—Publilius Syrus

It is better to err on the side of daring than the side of caution.

—Alvin Toffler

To achieve great things we must live as though we were never going to die. —Marquis de Vauvenargues

See also Courage; Fear; Risk

CHANGE

The main dangers in this life are the people who want to change everything . . . or nothing. —Lady Astor

He who will not apply new remedies must expect old evils.

—Francis Bacon

Things alter for the worse spontaneously, if they are not altered for the better designedly. —Francis Bacon

One does not fight to influence change and then leave the change to someone else to bring about. —Stokely Carmichael

When it is not necessary to change, it is necessary not to change. —Lucias Cary

Don't ever take a fence down until you know the reason why it was put up. —G. K. Chesterton

Life is not a static thing. The only people who do not change their minds are incompetents in asylums, who can't, and those in cemeteries. —Everett M. Dirksen

In every period of major transition, two kinds of leadership surface: those consumed by the threats of transition, and those open to the opportunities that always accompany transition. —William Easum

Fate cannot be changed; otherwise it would not be fate. Man, however, may well change himself, otherwise he would not be man. —Victor E. Frankl

When it comes to changes, people like only those that they make themselves. —French proverb

Nobody told me how hard and lonely change is.
—Joan Gilbertson

The longer we analyze the current ways of operating, the further we fend off that awesome day when we will have to change something. Analysis thus becomes a defensive maneuver to avoid making fundamental change.

— MICHAEL HAMMER AND STEVEN STANTON

There is no way to make people like change. You can only make them feel less threatened by it. — FREDERICK O'R. HAYES

Disorder at the top is perhaps the last thing people want to see when the distress of change compels them to seek greater reliability in their authorities. — RONALD A. HEIFETZ

In times of distress, people are often of mixed minds about change. They passionately want their lives to change and they look to figures of authority to take bold action to direct the change. Yet they also want the change to take place with a minimum of loss to them, and they look to authority for protection. — RONALD A. HEIFETZ

There is nothing permanent except change.

— HERACLITUS

We are more ready to try the untried when what we do is inconsequential. Hence the remarkable fact that many inventions had their birth as toys. — ERIC HOFFER

The vast majority of human beings dislike and even dread all notions with which they are not familiar. Hence it comes about that at their first appearance innovators have always been derided as fools and madmen. — ALDOUS HUXLEY

From Wall Street to Washington, from boardrooms to union halls, what anybody with power is most scared of is change. Any kind of change. Especially change that's forced on them.

—LEE IACCOCA

There is a certain relief in change, even though it be from bad to worse.

—WASHINGTON IRVING

Never underestimate the magnitude of the forces that reinforce complacency and help maintain the status quo.

— JOHN KOTTER

If you want to truly understand something, try to change it.

— KURT LEWIN

There is no sin punished more implacably by nature than the sin of resistance to change.

—ANNE MORROW LINDBERGH

There is nothing more difficult to take in hand, more perilous to conduct, or more uncertain in its success than to take the lead in introducing a new order of things.

—MACHIAVELLI

At every crossing on the road that leads to the future, each progressive spirit is opposed by a thousand appointed to guard the past.

—MAURICE MAETERLINCK

The philosophers have only interpreted the world; the thing, however, is to change it.

—KARL MARX

Every society honors its live conformists and its dead troublemakers.

—MIGNON MCLAUGHLIN

Change comes about when followers themselves desire it and seek it. Hence the role of the leader is to enlist the participation of others as leaders of the effort. That is the sum and essence not only of leading change but also of good management in general.
—JAMES O'TOOLE

Keep what you have; the known evil is best.

—PLAUTUS

In words as fashions the same rule will hold
    Alike fantastic if too new or old;
Be not the first by whom the new are tried,
    Nor yet the last to lay the old aside.

—ALEXANDER POPE

Happy he who learns to bear what he cannot change.
—JOHANN FRIEDRICH VON SCHILLER

All progress has resulted from people who took unpopular positions.
—ADLAI STEVENSON

Future shock [is] the shattering stress and disorientation that we induce in individuals by subjecting them to too much change in too short a time.
—ALVIN TOFFLER

Everybody thinks of changing humanity and nobody thinks of changing himself.
—LEO TOLSTOY

Most people are willing to change, not because they see the light but because they feel the heat.
—UNKNOWN

If the rate of change on the outside exceeds the rate of change on the inside, the end is near.
—JACK WELCH

The art of progress is to preserve order amid change and to preserve change amid order. — ALFRED NORTH WHITEHEAD

See also Action; Initiative; Open-mindedness

CHARACTER

Character is vital in the leader, the basis for everything else.
— WARREN BENNIS

Let us not say, Every man is the architect of his own fortune; but let us say, Every man is the architect of his own character.
— G. D. BOARDMAN

Someday, in years to come, you will be wrestling with the great temptation, or trembling under the great sorrow of your life. But the real struggle is here, now, in these quiet weeks. Now it is being decided whether, in the day of your supreme sorrow or temptation, you shall miserably fail or gloriously conquer. Character cannot be made except by a steady, long-continued process. —PHILLIPS BROOKS

Distance tests a horse's strength. Time reveals a man's character.
— CHINESE PROVERB

If you are standing upright, do not fear a crooked shadow.
— CHINESE PROVERB

Just as solid rocks are not shaken by the wind, so wise men are not moved by either blame or praise.
— DHAMMAPADA (THIRD CENTURY B.C. BUDDHIST ANTHOLOGY OF WISDOM)

Character isn't inherited. One builds it daily by the way one thinks and acts, thought by thought, action by action. If one lets fear or hate or anger take possession of the mind, they become self-forged chains. —HELEN DOUGLAS

Try not to become a person of success but rather a person of value. — ALBERT EINSTEIN

By nothing do men show their character more than by the things they laugh at. — JOHANN WOLFGANG VON GOETHE

No man knows of what stuff he is made until prosperity and ease try him. —A. P. GOUTHEY

The real test of a man is not when he plays the role that he wants for himself, but when he plays the role destiny has for him. —VACLAV HAVEL

The true test of character is not how much we know how to do, but how we behave when we don't know what to do. —JOHN HOLT

When the character of a man is not clear to you, look at his friends. —JAPANESE PROVERB

Character cannot be developed in ease and quiet. Only through experience of trial and suffering can the soul be strengthened, vision cleared, ambition inspired, and success achieved. —HELEN KELLER

If we are strong, our character will speak for itself. If we are weak, words will be of no help. —JOHN F. KENNEDY

Charisma without character leads to catastrophe.

— PETER KUZMIČ

Watch a man in times of . . . adversity to discover what kind of man he is; for then at last words of truth are drawn from the depths of his heart, and the mask is torn off . — LUCRETIUS

The measure of a man's real character is what he would do if he knew he would never be found out. — THOMAS MACAULAY

Some of necessity go astray, because for them there is no such thing as a right path. — THOMAS MANN

It is extraordinary how many emotional storms one may weather in safety if one is ballasted with ever so little gold.

— WILLIAM McFEE

If I take care of my character, my reputation will take care of itself. —DWIGHT L. MOODY

A disciplined conscience is a man's best friend. It may not be his most amiable, but it is his most faithful monitor.

—A. PHELPS

If I keep my good character, I shall be rich enough.

—PLATONICUS

Character is simply habit long continued.

—PLUTARCH

Men best show their character in trifles, where they are not on their guard. It is in insignificant matters, and in the simplest habits, that we often see the boundless egotism which pays no regard to the feelings of others, and denies nothing to itself.

—ARTHUR SCHOPENHAUER

Leadership consists of character and strategy. If you can't have both, opt for character. —NORMAN SCHWARZKOPF

To be worth anything, character must be capable of standing firm upon its feet in the world of daily work, temptation, and trial; and able to bear the wear and tear of actual life. Cloistered virtues do not count for much. —S. SMILES

Leadership . . . is both something you *are* and something you *do*. But effective leadership starts with character. When leaders fail, more often it is a result of a character flaw than a lack of competence. —FRED SMITH

One can acquire anything in solitude except character. —STENDHAL

Character consists of what you do on the third and fourth tries. —UNKNOWN

The best index to a person's character is (a) how he treats people who can't do him any good, and (b) how he treats people who can't fight back. —ABIGAIL VAN BUREN

If you refuse to be made straight when you are green, you will not be made straight when you are dry. — WEST AFRICAN PROVERB

Great occasions do not make heroes or cowards; they simply unveil them to the eyes of men. Silently and imperceptibly, as we wake or sleep, we grow strong or weak; and at last some crisis shows what we have become. —BROOKE FOSS WESTCOTT

Ability may get you to the top, but it takes character to keep you there. —JOHN WOODEN

If you wish to know what a man is, place him in authority.

— YUGOSLAV PROVERB

See also Individuality; Integrity and Reputation

CLEAR THINKING

Man is a creature of impulse, emotion, action rather than reason. Reason is a very late development in the world of living creatures, most of whom, as far as we know, get along admirably in daily life without it.　　　—JAMES T. ADAMS

Genius is the talent for seeing things straight. It is seeing things in a straight line without any bend or break or aberration of sight, seeing them as they are, without any warping of vision. Flawless sight! That is genius.　　　—MAUDE ADAMS

Genius is the ability to reduce the complicated to the simple.

—C. W. CERAM

It's always wise to raise questions about the most obvious and simple assumptions.　　　—C. WEST CHURCHMAN

Proof is often no more than lack of imagination—in providing an alternative explanation.　　　—EDWARD DE BONO

It is a capital mistake to theorize before one has data. Insensibly one begins to twist facts to suit theories, instead of theories to suit facts.　　　—ARTHUR CONAN DOYLE

When you have eliminated the impossible, whatever remains, however improbable, must be the truth.　　　—ARTHUR CONAN DOYLE

He who will not reason is a bigot; he who cannot is a fool; he who dares not is a slave. —WILLIAM DRUMMOND

When all else fails, people turn to reason.

—ABBA EBAN

Everything should be made as simple as possible, but not simpler. —ALBERT EINSTEIN

Neither great poverty nor great riches will hear reason.

—HENRY FIELDING

The test of a first-rate intelligence is the ability to hold two opposed ideas in mind at the same time and still retain the ability to function. —F. SCOTT FITZGERALD

If passion drives, let reason hold the reins.

—BENJAMIN FRANKLIN

Depend on it, when a man knows he is going to be hanged in a fortnight, it concentrates his mind wonderfully.

—SAMUEL JOHNSON

Your giving a reason for it will not make it right. You may have a reason why two and two make five, but they will still make but four. —SAMUEL JOHNSON

Ours is the age that is proud of machines that think and suspicious of men who try to. —H. MUMFORD JONES

No man's opinions are better than his information.

—ROBERT LENZNER

The spirit of the age is filled with disdain for thinking.

—ALBERT SCHWEITZER

It is better to know some of the questions than all of the answers. —JAMES THURBER

Far better an approximate answer to the right question, which is often vague, than an exact answer to the wrong question, which can always be made precise. —JOHN TUKEY

Individuals should be judged by their questions rather than by their answers. —VOLTAIRE

There are forty kinds of lunacy, but only one kind of common sense. —WEST AFRICAN PROVERB

It requires a very unusual mind to undertake the analysis of the obvious. —ALFRED NORTH WHITEHEAD

See also Ideas; Open-mindedness; Problems and Problem Solving

COMMUNICATION

In good communication, people should be in no doubt that you have reached a conclusion. —JOHN ADAIR AND NEIL THOMAS

As soon as you are complicated, you are ineffectual. — KONRAD ADENAUER

Hear the other side. — SAINT AUGUSTINE

Most of the successful people I've known are ones who do more listening than talking. . . . You don't have to blow out the other fellow's light to let your own shine. — BERNARD M. BARUCH

Effective leaders can communicate ideas through several organizational layers, across great distances, even through the jamming signals of special interest groups and opponents.

—WARREN BENNIS

Let your conversation be always full of grace, seasoned with salt, so that you may know how to answer everyone.

—THE BIBLE, COLOSSIANS 4:6

Even a fool is thought wise if he keeps silent, and discerning if he holds his tongue.

—THE BIBLE, PROVERBS 17:28

Nine-tenths of the serious controversies which result in life result from misunderstanding.

—LOUIS D. BRANDEIS

Never fail to know that if you are doing all the talking, you are boring somebody.

—HELEN GURLEY BROWN

Too much talk will include errors.

—BURMESE PROVERB

Silence is not always tact and it is tact that is golden, not silence.

—SAMUEL BUTLER

If you cry "Forward!" you must without fail make it plain in what direction to go. Don't you see that if, without doing so, you call out the word to both a monk and a revolutionary, they will go in directions precisely opposite?

—ANTON CHEKHOV

If you wish to know the mind of a man, listen to his speech.

—CHINESE PROVERB

If you have an important point to make, don't try to be subtle or clever. Use a pile driver. Hit the point once. Then come back and hit it again. Then hit it a third time—a tremendous whack.
—Winston Churchill

To persuade is more trouble than to dominate, and the powerful seldom take this trouble if they can avoid it.
—Charles Horton Cooley

Make thyself a craftsman in speech, for thereby thou shalt gain the upper hand.
—Egyptian tomb inscription

An intellectual is a man who takes more words than necessary to tell more than he knows.
—Dwight D. Eisenhower

I would rather persuade a man to go along, because once he has been persuaded he will stick. If I scare him, he will stay just as long as he is scared, and then he is gone.
—Dwight D. Eisenhower

It's said that Adlai Stevenson, when complimented on a speech, once pointed out that people often said what nice speeches he made, but that after John F. Kennedy's speeches they said, "Let's march!"
—Suzette Elgin

Be careful that you write accurately rather than much.
—Erasmus

Remember not only to say the right thing, in the right place, but far more difficult still to leave unsaid the wrong thing at the tempting moment.
—Benjamin Franklin

There is a time to say nothing, and a time to say something, but there is not time to say everything.
—Hugo of Fleury

Don't let your tongue say what your head may pay for.

—Italian proverb

A wise man hears one word and understands two.

— Jewish proverb

Zorba scratched his head. "I've got a thick skull, boss, I don't grasp these things easily. Ah, if only you could dance all that you have just said, then I'd understand. . . . Or if you would tell me all that in a story, boss." —Nikos Kazantzakis

Be different—if you don't have the facts and knowledge required, simply listen. When word gets around that you can listen when others tend to talk, you will be treated as a sage.

— Ed Koch

Wisdom is the reward you get for a lifetime of listening when you'd have preferred to talk. —Doug Larson

To write simply is as difficult as to be good.

— W. Somerset Maugham

Our capacity to communicate is beginning to totally overwhelm our ability to communicate with each other.

— Nancy Hicks Maynard

The point of good writing is knowing when to stop.

— L. M. Montgomery

We are drowning in information but starved for knowledge.

— John Naisbitt

Figure out what went wrong, not who was wrong, when communication breaks down. —Tom Nash

The best leaders . . . almost without exception and at every level, are master users of stories and symbols. —TOM PETERS

If my people understand me, I'll get their attention. If my people trust me, I'll get their action. —CAVETT ROBERTS

Big people monopolize the listening. Small people monopolize the talking. —DAVID SCHWARTZ

A sentence should contain no unnecessary words, a paragraph no unnecessary sentences, for the same reason that a drawing should have no unnecessary lines and a machine no unnecessary parts. —WILLIAM STRUNK JR. AND E. B. WHITE

Speech is not what one should desire to understand. One should know the speaker. —UPANISHAD

Communication is the art of being understood.
—PETER USTINOV

When we hear news we should always wait for the sacrament of confirmation. —VOLTAIRE

The key to success is to get out into the store and listen to what the associates have to say. It's terribly important for everyone to get involved. Our best ideas come from clerks and stockboys. —SAM WALTON

See also Media Relations; People Skills

COURAGE

It is easy to be brave from a distance.

—AESOP

Do not lay things too much to heart. No one is really beaten unless he is discouraged. —LORD AVEBURY

Courage is the thing. All goes if courage goes.

— J. M. BARRIE

Be strong and courageous. Do not be terrified; do not be discouraged, for the Lord your God will be with you wherever you go. —THE BIBLE, JOSHUA 1:9

Bravery is the capacity to perform properly even when scared half to death. —OMAR BRADLEY

Courage is almost a contradiction in terms. It means a strong desire to live taking the form of a readiness to die.

— G. K. CHESTERTON

Success is never final, failure is never fatal. It's courage that counts. —WINSTON CHURCHILL

The great need for anyone in authority is courage.

— ALISTAIR COOKE

Courage is contagious. When a brave man takes a stand, the spines of others are stiffened. —BILLY GRAHAM

Courage is grace under pressure.

— ERNEST HEMINGWAY

The test before us as a people is not whether our commitments match our will and our courage, but whether we have the will and the courage to match our commitments.

— LYNDON B. JOHNSON

To be courageous . . . requires no exceptional qualities, no magic formula, no special combination of time, place and circumstances. It is an opportunity that sooner or later is presented to us all.

—JOHN F. KENNEDY

Courage faces fear and thereby masters it. Cowardice represses fear and is thereby mastered by it.

— MARTIN LUTHER KING JR.

Perfect valor consists in doing without witnesses that which we would be capable of doing before everyone.

— DUC DE LA ROCHEFOUCAULD

I wanted you to see what real courage is, instead of getting the idea that courage is a man with a gun in his hand. It's when you know you're licked before you begin, but you begin anyway and you see it through no matter what.

— HARPER LEE, *To Kill a Mockingbird*

Courage is not simply *one* of the virtues but the form of every virtue at the testing point.

—C. S. LEWIS

Don't be afraid to take a big step if one is indicated. You can't cross a chasm in two small steps.

—DAVID LLOYD GEORGE

Courage is the ladder on which all other virtues mount.

— CLARE BOOTH LUCE

If you are brave too often, people will come to expect it of you.

—MIGNON MCLAUGLIN

The only courage that matters is the kind that gets you from one moment to the next. —MIGNON McLAUGLIN

Going through the necessary soul-searching of deciding whether to fight a battle, or to run away from it, is far more difficult than the battle itself. —RICHARD M. NIXON

Courage consists not in blindly overlooking danger, but in seeing it and conquering it. —JEAN PAUL RICHTER

Courage is doing what you're afraid to do. There can be no courage unless you're scared. —EDDIE RICKENBACKER

You must do the things you think you cannot do. —ELEANOR ROOSEVELT

Inactivity from fear of committing a fault is the mark of a coward. By whom is food renounced for fear of indigestion? —SANSKRIT PROVERB

Gloucester, 'tis true that we are in great danger;
The greater therefore should our courage be.
—WILLIAM SHAKESPEARE, *HENRY V*

Courage mounteth with occasion.
—WILLIAM SHAKESPEARE, *KING JOHN*

Screw your courage to the sticking place.
—WILLIAM SHAKESPEARE, *MACBETH*

A great deal of talent is lost in this world for want of a little courage. —SYDNEY SMITH

Keep your fears to yourself but share your courage.
—ROBERT LOUIS STEVENSON

It is curious that physical courage should be so common in the world and moral courage so rare. —MARK TWAIN

Courage is fear that has said its prayers.

— UNKNOWN

The test of courage comes when you are in the minority; the test of tolerance comes when you are in the majority.

— UNKNOWN

To fight a bull when you are not scared is nothing. And to not fight a bull when you are scared is nothing. But to fight a bull when you are scared—that is something.

— UNKNOWN BULLFIGHTER

See also Boldness; Fear; Risk

CREATIVITY

If you're not failing every now and again, it's a sign you're not being very innovative in what you're doing. —WESTON AGOR

We define genius as the capacity for productive reaction against one's training. —BERNARD BERENSON

Every great discovery I made, I gambled that the truth was there, and then I acted on it in faith until I could prove its existence. —ARTHUR H. COMPTON

Imagination is more important than knowledge.

— ALBERT EINSTEIN

Creative minds have always been known to survive any kind of bad training. —ANNA FREUD

The creative person is unique in that during the initial stages he prefers the chaotic and disorderly and tends to reject what has already been systematized. —RALPH J. HALLMAN

Every creative act requires elimination and simplification. Simplification results from a realization of what's essential. — HANS HOFFMANN

If you are seeking creative ideas, go out walking. Angels whisper to a man when he goes for a walk. —RAYMOND INMON

The uncreative mind can spot wrong answers, but it takes a creative mind to spot wrong questions. —ANTHONY JAY

The best way to have a good idea is to have a lot of ideas. —LINUS PAULING

Every act of creation is first an act of destruction. — PABLO PICASSO

The real act of discovery consists not in finding new lands but in seeing with new eyes. —MARCEL PROUST

The very essence of the creative is its novelty, and hence we have no standard by which to judge it. —CARL R. ROGERS

Resist the usual. — RAYMOND RUBICAM

Truly creative people use the gap between vision and current reality to generate energy for change. —PETER SENGE

Discovery consists of looking at the same thing as everyone else and thinking something different. — ALBERT SZENT-GYÖRGI

Don't refuse to go on an occasional wild goose chase. That's what wild geese are for. —UNKNOWN

Imagination was given to man to compensate for what he is not, and a sense of humor to console him for what he is.

— UNKNOWN

The amount a person uses his imagination is inversely proportional to the amount of punishment he will receive for using it.

— UNKNOWN

Creative people exhibit a continuous discontent with uniformity. —GLENN VAN EKEREN

The greatest invention of the nineteenth century was the invention of the method of invention.

— ALFRED NORTH WHITEHEAD

See also Problems and Problem Solving

CRISES

The Chinese write the word "crisis" with two characters. One means danger, and the other means opportunity. Together they spell "crisis." — SAUL D. ALINSKY (ALSO ATTRIBUTED TO OTHERS)

Never awake me when you have good news to announce, because with good news nothing presses; but when you have bad news, arouse me immediately, for then there is not an instant to be lost. — NAPOLEON BONAPARTE

Crises refine life. In them you discover what you are.

—ALLAN KNIGHT CHALMERS

To be mature means to face, and not evade, every fresh crisis that comes.

—FRITZ KUNKEL

It is by the presence of mind in untried emergencies that the native metal of a man is tested.

—JAMES RUSSELL LOWELL

In times of peril, like the needle to the lodestone, obedience, irrespective of rank, generally flies to him who is best to command.

—HERMAN MELVILLE

A leader or man of action in a crisis almost always acts subconsciously and then thinks of the reasons for his action.

—JAWAHARLAL NEHRU

The ability to be cool, confident, and decisive in crisis is not an inherited characteristic but is the direct result of how well the individual has prepared himself for the battle.

—RICHARD M. NIXON

The nearer any disease approaches to a crisis, the nearer it is to a cure.

—THOMAS PAINE

The ability to keep a cool head in an emergency, maintain poise in the midst of excitement and to refuse to be stampeded are true marks of leadership.

—R. SHANNON

To act coolly, intelligently and prudently in perilous circumstances is the test of a man—and also a nation.

—ADLAI STEVENSON

See also Pressures and Temptations

Critics are like eunuchs in a harem: they know how it's done, they've seen it done every day, but they're unable to do it themselves. —Brendan Behan

Men are not against you; they are merely for themselves.
— Gene Fowler

We must not in the course of public life expect immediate approbation and immediate grateful acknowledgment of our services. But let us persevere through abuse and even injury. The internal satisfaction of a good conscience is always present, and time will do us justice in the minds of the people, even those at present the most prejudiced against us.
— Benjamin Franklin

Any fool can criticize, and many of them do.
— Cyril Garbett

Correction does much, but encouragement does more. Encouragement after censure is as the sun after a shower.
— Johann Wolfgang von Goethe

We must touch his weaknesses with a delicate hand. There are some faults so nearly allied to excellence that we can scarce weed out the fault without eradicating the virtue.
— Oliver Goldsmith

Unless we are willing to help a person overcome his faults, there is little value in pointing them out.   — Robert J. Hastings

A critic is a man who expects miracles.
— James Gibbons Huneker

As a general rule, I abstain from reading the reports of attacks upon myself, wishing not to be provoked by that to which I cannot properly offer an answer. —ABRAHAM LINCOLN

He has a right to criticize, who has a heart to help. —ABRAHAM LINCOLN

I have never found, in a long experience of politics, that criticism is ever inhibited by ignorance. —HAROLD MACMILLAN

Conceal a flaw, and the world will imagine the worst. —MARTIAL

If it is very painful for you to criticize your friends, you are safe in doing it. But if you take the slightest pleasure in it, that is the time to hold your tongue. —ALICE MILLER

When a man is able to take abuse with a smile, he is worthy to become a leader. —NACHMAN OF BRASLAV

The trouble with most of us is that we would rather be ruined by praise than saved by criticism. —NORMAN VINCENT PEALE

If you are not criticized, you may not be doing much. —DONALD RUMSFELD

The foremost art of kings is the power to endure hatred. —SENECA (THE YOUNGER)

There is a kernel of truth in every criticism. Look for it, and when you find it, rejoice in its value. —DAWSON TROTMAN

A President may dismiss the abuse of scoundrels, but to be denounced by honest men honestly outraged is a test of greatness that none but the strongest men can survive.

— HARRY S. TRUMAN

A critic has been defined as someone who comes down from the mountain after the battle and shoots all the wounded.

— SANDER VANOCUR (ALSO ATTRIBUTED TO OTHERS)

Whatever you have to say to people, be sure to say it in words that will cause them to smile, and you will be on pretty safe ground. And when you do find it necessary to criticize someone, put your criticism in the form of a question which the other fellow is practically sure to have to answer in a manner that he becomes his own critic.

—JOHN WANAMAKER

You don't hear things that are bad about your company unless you ask. It is easy to hear good tidings, but you have to scratch to get the bad news.

—THOMAS J. WATSON JR.

DECISION MAKING

The man who insists upon seeing with perfect clearness before he decides, never decides.

—HENRI FREDERIC AMIEL

The fine art of executive decision making consists in not deciding questions that are not now pertinent, in not deciding prematurely, in not making decisions that cannot be made effective, and in not making decisions that others should make.

— CHESTER I. BARNARD

Harry, never display agony in public, in an opinion. Never display agony. Never say this is an agonizing, difficult decision. Always write it as though it's as clear as crystal.

—U.S. Supreme Court Justice Hugo Black to
fellow Justice Harry Blackmun

Nothing is more difficult, and therefore more precious, than to be able to decide. —Napoleon Bonaparte

We make our decisions, and then our decisions turn around and make us. —F. W. Boreham

I don't know what a hard decision is. Whenever I make a decision, I start out by recognizing that there's a strong likelihood that I'm going to be wrong. All I can do is the best I can. To worry about it puts obstacles in the way of clear thinking.

—Fletcher Byrom

Chi Wen Tzu always thought three times before taking action. Twice would have been quite enough. —Confucius

Not to decide is to decide.

— Harvey Cox

The importance of a decision is not what it will cost but how difficult it will be to reverse. —Peter Drucker

If you wish to avoid making a decision, either send a memo . . . or set up a committee to conduct an "in-depth study." —Epson's Compleat Office Companion

When it is not necessary to make a decision, it is necessary not to make a decision. —Lord Falkland

Soon after a heart-wrung decision something inevitably occurs to cast doubt on your choice. Holding steady against that doubt usually proves your decision.   —R. I. FITZHENRY

When making a decision of minor importance I have always found it advantageous to consider all the pros and cons. In vital matters, however, such as the choice of a mate or a profession, the decisions should come from the unconscious, from somewhere within ourselves. In the important decisions of our personal lives we should be governed by the deep inner needs of our nature.   —SIGMUND FREUD

Countless questions about a decision's immediate and ultimate consequences can be avoided by testing each alternative this way: does it fit my ethical framework?
   —ROBERT GILBREATH

When possible make the decisions now, even if action is in the future. A reviewed decision usually is better than one reached at the last moment.   —WILLIAM B. GIVEN

With every decision you make, no matter how small or large, you are making a statement about what matters to you.
   — DAVID P. HELFAND

What the hell—you might be right, you might be wrong . . . but don't just avoid it.   —KATHARINE HEPBURN

My basic principle is that you don't make decisions because they are easy, you don't make them because they are cheap, you don't make them because they are popular; you make them because they are right. Not distinguishing between rightness and wrongness is where administrators get into trouble.   —THEODORE HESBURGH

Indecision is debilitating; it feeds upon itself. It is, one might almost say, habit-forming. Not only that, but it is contagious; it transmits itself to others. . . . Often greater risk is involved in postponement than in making a wrong decision.

—HARRY A. HOPF

Take time to deliberate, but when the time for action arrives, stop thinking and go in. —ANDREW JACKSON

There is no more miserable human being than one in whom nothing is habitual but indecision. —WILLIAM JAMES

If I wasn't making mistakes, I wasn't making decisions.

— ROBERT W. JOHNSON, FOUNDER OF JOHNSON & JOHNSON

High office teaches decision making, not substance. [It] consumes intellectual capital; it does not create it. Most high officials leave office with the perceptions and insights with which they entered; they learn how to make decisions but not what decisions to make. —HENRY KISSINGER

The statesman must weigh the rewards of success against the penalties of failure. And he is permitted only one guess.

— HENRY KISSINGER

In the end the fundamental decisions a leader makes are decisions of character. —ALEX KROLL

The business executive is by profession a decision maker. Uncertainty is his opponent. Overcoming it is his mission. Whether the outcome is a consequence of luck or of wisdom, the moment of decision is without doubt the most creative and critical event in the life of the executive.

— JOHN MCDONALD

The manager has to live with a life in which he never really gets the luxury of choosing between right and wrong. He has to decide usually between two wrongs. In any decision he makes, he hurts somebody. And that's his career. If he's too uncomfortable with that, he ought to be in some other business. Obviously he ought to be uncomfortable with it. If he isn't uncomfortable, he's not very human. —J. IRWIN MILLER

The executive's loneliest hours are spent in choosing, not between right and wrong, but between two rights or two wrongs. His most creative moments are those in which he successfully integrates values, bringing diverse ideas together into new arrangements. —DAVID G. MOORE

I have an absolute rule. I refuse to make a decision that somebody else can make. The first rule of leadership is to save yourself for the big decision. Don't allow your mind to become cluttered with the trivia. Don't let yourself become the issue.
—RICHARD M. NIXON

The man who is denied the opportunity of taking decisions of importance begins to regard as important the decisions he is allowed to take. —C. NORTHCOTE PARKINSON

The best decision-makers are those who are willing to suffer the most over their decisions but still retain their ability to be decisive. —M. SCOTT PECK

I think working hard to make a decision work is possibly even more important than making the decision in the first place. One of the dangers is people making a decision then thinking, "Oh, that's it," when the thing has only just started.
—LORD PENNOCK

I've never taken a major decision without consulting my colleagues. It would be unimaginable to me, unimaginable. First, they help me to make a better decision in most cases. Second, if they know about it and agree with it, they'll back it. Otherwise, they might challenge it, not openly, but subconsciously. —ALASTAIR PILKINGTON

There is a time when we must firmly choose the course we will follow, or the relentless drift of events will make the decision. —HERBERT V. PROCHNOW

A decision is the action an executive must take when he has information so incomplete that the answer does not suggest itself. —ARTHUR W. RADFORD

In any moment of decision the best thing you can do is the right thing, the next best thing is the wrong thing, and the worst thing you can do is nothing. —THEODORE ROOSEVELT

The executive's job involves not only making decisions himself, but also seeing that the organization, or part of an organization, that he directs makes decisions effectively. The vast bulk of the decision-making activity for which he is responsible is not his personal activity, but the activity of his subordinates.

—H. A. SIMON

No one learns to make right decisions without being free to make wrong ones. —KENNETH SOLLITT

All decisions should be made as low as possible in the organization. The charge of the Light Brigade was ordered by an officer who wasn't looking at the territory.

—ROBERT TOWNSEND

Once a decision was made, I did not worry about it afterward.

—HARRY S. TRUMAN

Making up your mind is the hard part—the rest is just pure work.

—UNKNOWN

When you know what your values are, making decisions becomes easier.

—GLENN VAN EKEREN

The more decisions that you are forced to make alone, the more you are aware of your freedom to choose. I hold that we cannot be said to be aware of our minds save under responsibility.

—THORNTON WILDER

Keep focused on the substantive issues. To make a decision means having to go through one door and closing all others.

—ABRAHAM ZALEZNIK

DIFFICULTIES

I am not afraid of storms for I am learning how to sail my ship.

—LOUISA MAY ALCOTT

Sunshine without rain is the recipe for a desert.

—ARABIAN PROVERB

Adversity has the same effect on a man that severe training has on the pugilist—it reduces him to his fighting weight.

— JOSH BILLINGS

God knows exactly how to get you out of trouble. He has not forgotten how to part the sea.

—LYNNE BUNDESEN

It is the character of a brave and resolute man not to be ruffled by adversity and not to desert his post.   —CICERO

A man of character finds a special attractiveness in difficulty, since it is only by coming to grips with difficulty that he can realize his potentialities.   —CHARLES DE GAULLE

There is no education like adversity.

—BENJAMIN DISRAELI

Obstacles are those frightful things you see when you take your eyes off your goal.   —HENRY FORD

When you encounter difficulties and contradictions, do not try to break them, but bend them with gentleness and time.

—SAINT FRANCIS DE SALES

The greatest difficulties lie where we are not looking for them.

—JOHANN WOLFGANG VON GOETHE

Prosperity is a great teacher; adversity is a greater. Possession pampers the mind; privation trains and strengthens it.

—WILLIAM HAZLITT

Adversity has the effect of eliciting talents which in prosperous circumstances would have lain dormant.   —HORACE

The first rule of holes: When you're in one, stop digging.

—MOLLY IVINS

Adversity is the state in which a man most easily becomes acquainted with himself, being especially free from admirers then.   —SAMUEL JOHNSON

Difficulty is for the most part the daughter of idleness.

—SAMUEL JOHNSON

He knows not his own strength who hath not met adversity.

— BEN JONSON

No one would have crossed the ocean if he could have gotten off the ship in the storm. — CHARLES F. KETTERING

With me a change of trouble is as good as a vacation.

— DAVID LLOYD GEORGE

People don't seem to realize that doing what's right's no guarantee against misfortune. —WILLIAM MCFEE

Before you begin a thing, remind yourself that difficulties and delays quite impossible to foresee are ahead. If you could see them clearly, naturally you could do a great deal to get rid of them but you can't. You can only see one thing clearly and that is your goal. Form a mental vision of that and cling to it through thick and thin. —KATHLEEN THOMPSON NORRIS

When a piece gets difficult, make faces.

— ARTUR SCHNABEL, PIANIST

I will be courageous and undismayed in the face of odds. I will not permit anyone to intimidate me or deter me from my goals. I will take new faith and resolution from the knowledge that all successful men and women had to fight despair and adversity. I will never surrender to discouragement or despair, no matter what seeming obstacles may confront me. — HAROLD SHERMAN

See also Crises; Goals; Problems and Problem Solving; Pressures and Temptations

EFFORT AND WORK

Work is good, provided you do not forget to live.

— BANTU PROVERB

Nothing is really work unless you would rather be doing something else. —J. M. BARRIE

Whatever your hand finds to do, do it with all your might.

— THE BIBLE, ECCLESIASTES 9:10

There is an important clue as to whether one is carrying out good work. Doing good work feels good. Few things in life are as enjoyable as when we concentrate on a difficult task, using all our skills, knowing what had to be done.

— HOWARD GARDNER, MIHALY CSIKSZENTMIHALYI, AND WILLIAM DAMON

The things, good Lord, that we pray for, give us the grace to labor for. —THOMAS MORE

I loathe drudgery as much as any man; but I have learned that the only way to conquer drudgery is to get through it as neatly, as efficiently, as one can. . . . A dull job slackly done becomes twice as dull, whereas a dull job which you try to do just as well as you can becomes half as dull.

—HAROLD NICOLSON

Happiness doesn't come from doing what we like to do but from liking what we have to do. —WILFRED PETERSON

In order that people may be happy in their work, these three things are needed: they must be fit for it; they must not do too much of it; and they must have a sense of success in it.

— JOHN RUSKIN

One of the symptoms of an approaching nervous breakdown is the belief that one's work is terribly important.

— BERTRAND RUSSELL

God performs the impossible; the possible we are required and obligated to do ourselves. — UNKNOWN

O Lord, thou givest us everything at the price of an effort.

— LEONARDO DA VINCI

Ask God's blessing on your work but do not also ask Him to do it. —WAGGERL

See also Action; Initiative

ENTHUSIASM

The energy that makes organizations move depends upon individual enthusiasm. Leaders with bright ideas and the ability to inspire high thought and action in others are the main generators of energy. Their individual brand of enthusiasm rubs off onto other people and inspires them to greater works.

— BRIAN ADAMS

If you can give your son only one gift, let it be enthusiasm.

— BRUCE BARTON

If I am trying to decide between two men of fairly equal ability and one man definitely has enthusiasm, I know he will go further, for enthusiasm has self-releasing power and carries all before it. —WALTER CHRYSLER

Nothing great was ever achieved without enthusiasm.

— RALPH WALDO EMERSON

Practice being excited.

— BILL FOSTER

Jingshen is the Mandarin word for spirit and vivacity. It is an important word for those who would lead, because above all things, spirit and vivacity set effective organizations apart from those that will decline and die. — JAMES L. HAYES

The good leader is not ashamed of the fact that he is an enthusiast. He knows intuitively that he has to be one. His zeal is in large part the measure of his influence. Ultimately, such impelling enthusiasm is related also to the basic life faith or outlook which one holds. The pessimist, the cynic or the nihilist is no enthusiast. — TEAD ORDWAY

Once we have made enthusiasm ridiculous, there is nothing left but money and power. — MADAME DE STAËL

Apathy can only be overcome by enthusiasm, and enthusiasm can only be aroused by two things: first, an ideal which takes the imagination by storm, and second, a definite intelligible plan for carrying that ideal into practice. — ARNOLD TOYNBEE

No one keeps up his enthusiasm automatically. Enthusiasm must be nourished with new actions, new aspirations, new efforts, new vision. It is one's own fault if his enthusiasm is gone; he has failed to feed it. — UNKNOWN

EXCELLENCE

Excellence . . . is not an act, but a habit.

— ARISTOTLE

Striving for excellence motivates you; striving for perfection is demoralizing.

— HARRIET BRAIKER

The only thing that separates any one of us from excellence is fear, and the opposite of fear is faith. I am careful not to confuse excellence with perfection. Excellence I can reach for, perfection is God's business.

— MICHAEL J. FOX

Some people have greatness thrust upon them. Very few have excellence thrust upon them.

— JOHN W. GARDNER

Be a yardstick of quality. Some people aren't used to an environment where excellence is expected.

— STEPHEN JOBS

The achievement of excellence requires great effort, much planning, and even more time. But, in the long run, mediocrity costs more, drains your energy, and wastes even more time than it takes to do things right.

— NORMAN LAMM

The quality of a man's life is in direct proportion to his commitment to excellence.

— TOM LANDRY

Only a mediocre person is always at his best.

— W. SOMERSET MAUGHAM

Excellent things are rare.

— PLATO

Excellence is the gradual result of always striving to do better.

—Pat Riley

Don't be afraid to give up the good to go for the great.

—Kenny Rogers

It takes a long time to bring excellence to maturity.

—Publilius Syrus

Excellence, to me, is the state of grace that can descend only when one tunes out all the world's clamor, listens to an inward voice one recognizes as wiser than one's own, and transcribes without fear.   —Naomi Wolf

EXPERIENCE

All experience is an arch, to build upon.

—Henry Adams

Experience has no text books nor proxies. She demands that her pupils answer her roll-call personally.   —Minna Antrim

Ask the experienced rather than the learned.

—Arabian proverb

Man arrives as a novice at each age of his life.

—Nicolas Chamfort

Experience is a comb that nature gives us when we are bald.

—Chinese proverb (also attributed to other nationalities)

Information's pretty thin stuff, unless mixed with experience.
— CLARENCE DAY

Experience keeps a dear school, yet fools will learn in no other.
— BENJAMIN FRANKLIN

It's taken me all my life to learn what not to play.
— DIZZY GILLESPIE

Experience is not what happens to you; it is what you do with what happens to you.
— ALDOUS HUXLEY

Experience enables you to recognize a mistake when you make it again.
— FRANKLIN P. JONES

Experience is a hard teacher because she gives the test first, the lesson afterwards.
— VERNON LAW

Do not look where you fell, but where you slipped.
— LIBERIAN PROVERB

He who neglects to drink of the spring of experience is apt to die of thirst in the desert of ignorance.
— LING PO

One thorn of experience is worth a whole wilderness of warning.
— JAMES RUSSELL LOWELL

A person who has had a bull by the tail once has learned sixty or seventy times as much as a person who hasn't.
— MARK TWAIN

We should be careful to get out of an experience only the wisdom that is in it—and stop there, lest we be like the cat that sits down on a hot stove-lid. She will never sit down on a hot stove-lid again, and that is well; but also she will never sit down on a cold one anymore. — MARK TWAIN

Experience is like drawing without an eraser.

— UNKNOWN

Experience is the name everyone gives to their mistakes.

— OSCAR WILDE

We learn from experience. A man never wakes up his second baby just to see it smile. — GRACE WILLIAMS

See also Failure; Mistakes

FAILURE

Whenever you fall, pick something up.

— OSWALD AVERY

If at first you don't succeed, try, try again. Then quit. There's no use being a damn fool about it. — W. C. FIELDS

Failure is only the opportunity to begin again more intelligently. — HENRY FORD

Almost as many individuals fail because they try to do too much as fail because they do not do enough.

— J. PAUL GETTY

It is possible to defeat failure by analyzing its causes and correcting them, not by studying the conditions of success.

— HENRY GREBER

A failure is a man who has blundered but is not able to cash in on the experience.

— ELBERT HUBBARD

Once you've failed, analyze the problem and find out why, because each failure is one more step leading up to the cathedral of success. The only time you don't want to fail is the last time you try.

— CHARLES F. KETTERING

You need the ability to fail. I'm amazed at the number of organizations that set up an environment where they do not permit their people to be wrong. You cannot innovate unless you are willing to accept some mistakes.

— CHARLES KNIGHT

Sometimes it is more important to discover what one cannot do than what one can do.

— LIN YUTANG

In great attempts it is glorious even to fail.

— LONGINUS

Not failure, but low aim, is crime.

— JAMES RUSSELL LOWELL

Defeat may serve as well as victory to shake the soul and let the glory out.

— EDWIN MARKHAM

Failure can be divided into those who thought and never did and into those who did and never thought.

— W. A. NANCE

Good people are good because they've come to wisdom through failure. We get very little wisdom from success.

— WILLIAM SAROYAN

When I was a young man I observed that nine out of ten things I did were failures. I didn't want to be a failure, so I did ten times more work. — GEORGE BERNARD SHAW

I cannot give you the formula for success, but I can give you the formula for failure: Try to please everybody.
— HERBERT BAYER SWOPE

It's a lonesome walk to the sidelines, especially when thousands of people are cheering your replacement.
— FRAN TARKENTON

In the game of life it's a good idea to have a few early losses, which relieves you of the pressure of trying to maintain an undefeated season. — BILL VAUGHAN

We are not interested in the possibilities of defeat; they do not exist. — QUEEN VICTORIA

In God's economy, nothing is wasted. Through failure, we learn a lesson in humility which is probably needed, painful though it is. — BILL WILSON

See also Experience; Success

FAME AND RECOGNITION

Fame always brings loneliness. Success is as ice cold and lonely as the north pole. — VICKI BAUM

Applause is the spur of noble minds, the end and aim of weak ones. — CHARLES CALEB COLTON

No person was ever honored for what he received. Honor has been the reward for what he gave. — CALVIN COOLIDGE

Fame is a food that dead men eat,
I have no stomach for such meat.

— HENRY AUSTIN DOBSON

Fame is based on what people say about you, reputation on what they think of you. — LOUIS DUDEK

Those only deserve a monument who do not need one.

— WILLIAM HAZLITT

Fame usually comes to those who are thinking about something else. — OLIVER WENDELL HOLMES SR.

You may succeed in the lower sense of that word. You may become rich; may come to be the first man in a village, or a member of Congress, or the governor of a state, or the president of the United States, and may suppose yourselves to be engaged, as ten thousand have before you, in the most important and momentous concerns that have ever transpired. But, however high you may rise, you will be borne up by a wave that has risen quite as high before, and when it subsides it will strand you where it has stranded others, and leave you to neglect, while the popular gaze is waiting for him who is to succeed you.

— MARK HOPKINS, PRESIDENT OF WILLIAMS COLLEGE;
COMMENCEMENT ADDRESS, 1872

Fame and tranquility are two things that can't live under the same roof. — MICHEL DE MONTAIGNE

Applause. Enjoy it, but never quite believe it.

— ROBERT MONTGOMERY

Fame is something which must be won; honor only something which must not be lost.   — ARTHUR SCHOPENHAUER

Wealth is like sea-water: the more we drink, the thirstier we become; and the same is true of fame.

— ARTHUR SCHOPENHAUER

There is no question you get pumped up by the recognition. Then a self-loathing sets in when you realize you're enjoying it.   — GEORGE C. SCOTT

What a heavy burden is a name that has too soon become famous.   — VOLTAIRE

See also Ambition—Promise and Pitfalls; Humility

FEAR

No passion so effectually robs the mind of all its powers of acting and reasoning as fear.   — EDMUND BURKE

Forget the self and you will fear nothing.

— CARLOS CASTANEDA

"The trouble is, Sancho," said Don Quixote, "you are so afraid that you cannot see or hear properly; for one of the effects of fear is to disturb the senses and cause things to appear other than they are."   — MIGUEL DE CERVANTES

Nothing in life is to be feared. It is only to be understood.

— MARIE CURIE

The first and great commandment is, don't let them scare you.

— ELMER DAVIS

Fear always springs from ignorance.

— RALPH WALDO EMERSON

A good scare is worth more to a man than good advice.

— ED HOWE

We fear things in proportion to our ignorance of them.

— LIVY

There is no passion so contagious as that of fear.

— MICHEL DE MONTAIGNE

The time to take counsel of your fears is before you make an important battle decision. That's the time to listen to every fear you can imagine! When you have collected all the facts and fears and made your decision, turn off all your fears and go ahead!

— GEORGE S. PATTON

I made the decision long ago that to be afraid would be to diminish my life.

— JANET RENO

Of all the passions, fear weakens judgment most.

— CARDINAL DE RETZ

Let me assert my firm belief that the only thing we have to fear is fear itself.

— FRANKLIN D. ROOSEVELT

Fear makes men believe the worst.

— QUINTUS RUFUS

He must necessarily fear many, whom many fear.

— SENECA (ALSO ATTRIBUTED TO OTHERS)

A frightened captain makes a frightened crew.

— LISTER SINCLAIR

To the man who is afraid everything rustles.

— SOPHOCLES

Three fears weaken the heart: fear of the truth, fear of poverty, and fear of the devil. — WELSH PROVERB

See also Boldness; Courage; Risk

FOLLOWERS

A political leader must keep looking over his shoulder all the time to see if the boys are still there. If they aren't still there, he's no longer a political leader. — BERNARD M. BARUCH

The crowd will follow a leader who marches twenty paces ahead of them, but if he is a thousand paces ahead of them, they will neither see nor follow him. — GEORG BRANDES

All organizations, nations, societies, and civilizations will prosper and advance only to the extent that they can encourage common men to perform uncommon deeds.

— COURTNEY C. BROWN

The signs of outstanding leadership are found among the followers. —MAX DEPREE

People are more easily led than driven.

— DAVID HAROLD FINK

The only test of leadership is that somebody follows.

— ROBERT GREENLEAF

He who thinketh he leadeth and hath no one following him is only taking a walk.

—BENJAMIN HOOKS

Followership is not a person but a role, and what distinguishes followers from leaders is not intelligence or character but the role they play. . . . Effective followers and effective leaders are often the same people playing different parts at different parts of the day.

— ROBERT E. KELLEY

Leaders matter greatly. But in searching so zealously for better leaders we tend to lose sight of the people these leaders will lead. Without his armies, Napoleon was just a man with grandiose ambitions. Organizations stand or fall partly on the basis of how well their leaders lead, but partly also on the basis of how well their followers follow.

— ROBERT E. KELLEY

To lead, one must follow.

— LAO-TZU

Remember that it is far better to follow well than to lead indifferently.

—JOHN G. VANCE

FUNDAMENTALS

If you must play, decide on three things at the start: the rules of the game, the stakes, and the quitting time.

— CHINESE PROVERB

Many people fail simply because they conclude that fundamentals simply do not apply in their case. —M. L. CICHON

Begin with the end in mind.

—STEPHEN R. COVEY

I soon learned to scent out that which was able to lead to fundamentals and to turn aside everything else, from the multitude of things that clutter up the mind, and divert it from the essential. —ALBERT EINSTEIN

Play the game right. If you play the game intelligently and execute the fundamentals, you can win. —TONY LARUSSA

One of the disciplines of building a rich soul life seems to be the simple act, on a daily basis, of remembering what is most important to us. —DAVID WHYTE

See also Goals; Priorities

THE FUTURE

Never let the future disturb you. You will meet it, if you have to, with the same weapons of reason which today arm you against the present. —MARCUS AURELIUS

Men must pursue things which are just in the present and leave the future to the divine Providence. —FRANCIS BACON

Do not boast about tomorrow, for you do not know what a day may bring forth. —THE BIBLE, PROVERBS 27:1

Destiny is not a matter of chance, it is a matter of choice; it is not a thing to be waited for, it is a thing to be achieved.

—WILLIAM JENNINGS BRYAN

You can never plan the future by the past.

— EDMUND BURKE

To know the road ahead, ask those coming back.

— CHINESE PROVERB

It is a mistake to look too far ahead. Only one link of the chain of destiny can be handled at a time.

—WINSTON CHURCHILL

What we look for does not come to pass. God finds a way for what none foresaw.

— EURIPIDES

The future is a mirror without any glass in it.

— XAVIER FORNERET

People often overestimate what will happen in the next two years, and underestimate what will happen in the next ten.

— BILL GATES

It's difficult to unlearn behaviors that made us successful in the past—speaking rather than listening; valuing people like yourself over people of different genders or from different cultures; doing things on your own rather than collaborating; making the decision yourself instead of asking different people for their perspectives. There's a whole range of behaviors that were highly functional in the hierarchical organization that are dead wrong in the flatter, more responsive, empowered organization that we're seeking to become.

— ROBERT HAAS

The only way to predict the future is to have the power to shape the future. —ERIC HOFFER

Do not try to find out—we're forbidden to know—what end the gods have in store for me, or for you. —HORACE

Pick today's fruits, not relying on the future in the slightest. —HORACE

The future is something which everyone reaches at the rate of sixty minutes an hour, whatever he does, whoever he is. —C. S. LEWIS

Unless we can find some way to keep our sights on tomorrow, we cannot expect to be in touch with today. —DEAN RUSK

Where there's no faith in the future, there's no power in the present. —UNKNOWN

It is the business of the future to be dangerous. —ALFRED NORTH WHITEHEAD

Progress imposes not only new possibilities for the future, but new restrictions. —NORBERT WIENER

There are no stains on the pages of tomorrow. —GRADY B. WILSON

GOALS

If we have not achieved our early dreams, we must either find new ones or see what we can salvage from the old. If we have accomplished what we set out to do in our youth, then we need not weep like Alexander the Great that we have no more worlds to conquer. There is clearly much left to be done, and whatever else we are going to do, we had better get on with it.
—Rosalynn Smith Carter

Along this track of pathless ocean it is my intention to steer.
—Christopher Columbus

Arriving at one goal is the starting point to another.
—John Dewey

A goal is nothing more than a dream with a time limit.
—Joe L. Griffith

Never look down to test the ground before taking your next step; only he who keeps his eye fixed on the far horizon will find his right road.
—Dag Hammarskjöld

Aim at the sun, and you may not reach it; but your arrow will fly far higher than if aimed at an object on a level with yourself.
—J. Hawes

My greatest fear for you is not that you will fail but that you will succeed in doing the wrong thing.
—Howard Hendricks

If you hit every time, the target is too near or too big.
—Tom Hirshfield

Efforts and courage are not enough without purpose and direction.
                                                    —John F. Kennedy

It must be borne in mind that the tragedy of life doesn't lie in not reaching your goal. The tragedy lies in having no goal to reach.
                                                    —Benjamin E. Mays

Lord, grant that I may always desire more than I can accomplish.
                                                    —Michelangelo

Get your major purpose clear, take off your plate all which hinders that purpose and hold hard to all that helps it, and then go ahead with a clear conscience, courage, sincerity, and selflessness.
                                                    —Bernard L. Montgomery

Providence has nothing good or high in store for one who does not resolutely aim at something high or good. A purpose is the eternal condition of success.
                                                    —T. T. Munger

It's more important to have great goals, than great goal statements.
                                                    —Shaun Murphy

You must have long-range goals to keep you from being frustrated by short-range failures.
                                                    —Charles C. Noble

If you don't know where you are going, you will end up somewhere else.
                                                    —Laurence Peter

I don't set goals for other people. That is one of their key jobs —to define their goals, to define success. I set goals for myself, but not for other people.
                                                    —Alastair Pilkington

Let us not dedicate ourselves to useless battles and the striving after goals impossible to attain. Let us follow the lighted star. Let us seek what is reasonable, not waste our courage on a struggle for dreams.   — Luis Muñoz Rivera

More men fail through lack of purpose than through lack of talent.   — Billy Sunday

In the long run, men hit only what they aim at.

— Henry David Thoreau

Having lost sight of our goals, we've decided to redouble our efforts.   — Unknown

See also Vision

HOPE AND DESPAIR

Never despair; but if you do, work on in despair.

— Edmund Burke

Those who have much to hope and nothing to lose will always be dangerous.   — Edmund Burke

Despair is presumption, pure and simple, a going beyond what the facts at hand warrant. . . . The worst thing is never the last thing. God is already working on Plan B even as Plan A lies in shambles around our feet.   — John Claypool

The hope is always here, always alive, but only your fierce caring can fan it into a fire to warm the world.   — Susan Cooper

No one has a right to sit down and feel hopeless. There's too much work to do. — DOROTHY DAY

Hope is one of the principal springs that keep mankind in motion. — ANDREW FULLER

The first and last task of a leader is to keep hope alive.
— JOHN W. GARDNER

In all things it is better to hope than to despair.
— JOHANN WOLFGANG VON GOETHE

Hope is a pleasant acquaintance, but an unsafe friend; not the man for your banker, though he may do for a traveling companion. — THOMAS HALIBURTON

A propensity to hope and joy is real riches; one to fear and sorrow, real poverty. — DAVID HUME

Where there is no hope, there can be no endeavor.
— SAMUEL JOHNSON

Hope is the feeling you have [that] the feeling you have isn't permanent. — JEAN KERR

Hope is the ability to listen to the music of the future. Faith is the courage to dance to it in the present. — PETER KUZMIČ

We promise according to our hopes, and perform according to our fears. — DUC DE LA ROCHEFOUCAULD

Everything that is done in the world is done by hope. No husbandman would sow one grain of corn if he hoped not it would grow up and become seed; no bachelor would marry a wife if he hoped not to have children; no merchant or tradesman would set himself to work if he did not hope to reap benefit thereby. — MARTIN LUTHER

Despair is the one sin that cannot be forgiven.

— NGUGI WA THIONG'O

Hope springs eternal in the human breast.

— ALEXANDER POPE

It is at night that faith in light is admirable.

— EDMOND ROSTAND

Hope is putting faith to work when doubting would be easier. — UNKNOWN

HUMILITY

The greater you are, the more you must practice humility.

— THE APOCRYPHA

Life is a long lesson in humility.

— J. M. BARRIE

It is no great thing to be humble when you are brought low; but to be humble when you are praised is a great and rare attainment. — SAINT BERNARD OF CLAIRVAUX

It is part of the discipline of humility that we must not spare our hand where it can perform a service and that we do not assume that our schedule is our own to manage, but allow it to be arranged by God. — DIETRICH BONHOEFFER

The true way to be humble is not to stoop until you are smaller than yourself, but to stand at your real height against some higher nature that will show you what the real smallness of your greatness is. — PHILLIPS BROOKS

Humility is not a weak and timid quality; it must be carefully distinguished from a groveling spirit. There is such a thing as an honest pride and self-respect. Though we may be servants of all, we should be servile to none. — E. H. CHAPIN

It is always the secure who are humble.

— G. K. CHESTERTON

Always remember that there are two types of people in this world. Those who come into a room and say, "Well, here I am!" and those who come in and say, "Ah, there you are!"

— FREDERICK L. COLLINS

A sense of humility is a quality I have observed in every leader I have deeply admired. — DWIGHT D. EISENHOWER

Humility is the most difficult of all virtues to achieve; nothing dies harder than the desire to think well of oneself.

— T. S. ELIOT

Most of the trouble in the world is caused by people wanting to be important. — T. S. ELIOT

Humility in the more powerful is ultimately tested by their ability to learn from, and gratefully to receive the gifts of, the less powerful. — ROBERT GREENLEAF

True merit, like a river, the deeper it is, the less noise it makes. — CHARLES MONTAGU HALIFAX

Teach thy tongue to say: "I do not know." — HEBREW PROVERB

Young man, the secret of my success is that at an early age I discovered I was not God. — OLIVER WENDELL HOLMES JR.

Use your light, but dim your brightness. — LAO-TZU

A humble man can do great things with an uncommon perfection because he is no longer concerned about accidentals, like his own interests and his own reputation, and therefore, he is no longer needing to waste his efforts in defending them. — THOMAS MERTON

Let us be a little humble; let us think that the truth may not perhaps be entirely with us. — JAWAHARLAL NEHRU

All greatness grows great by self-abasement, and not by exalting itself. — NESTORIUS

Avoid having your ego so close to your position that when your position falls, your ego goes with it. — COLIN POWELL

The first test of a really great man is his humility. — JOHN RUSKIN

Really great men have a curious feeling that the greatness is not in them but through them. — JOHN RUSKIN

Humility is to make a right estimate of one's self.
— CHARLES HADDON SPURGEON

Humility is nothing but the truth. Humility is a synonym for honesty, not hypocrisy. It is not an artificial pretense about myself, but an accurate assessment of myself. — JOHN STOTT

Be humble, that you may not be humbled.
— THE TALMUD

Whoever humbles himself, God elevates him; whoever is proud, God brings him down. Whoever runs after honors, honors run away from him. — THE TALMUD

If you are humble, nothing will touch you, neither praise nor disgrace, because you know what you are. — MOTHER TERESA

A fault which humbles a man is of more use to him than a good action which puffs him up. — THOMAS WILSON

See also Ambition—Promise and Pitfalls

IDEAS

History marches to the drum of a clear idea.
— W. H. AUDEN

Nothing is more dangerous than an idea when it is the only one you have. — EMILE CHARTIER

A good idea needs landing gear as well as wings.
— KEN EDGECOMBE

Daring ideas are like chessmen moved forward; they may be beaten but they may start a winning game.
— JOHANN WOLFGANG VON GOETHE

Man's mind, stretched to a new idea, never goes back to its original dimension.
— OLIVER WENDELL HOLMES JR.

Many ideas grow better when transplanted into another mind than in the one where they sprang up.
— OLIVER WENDELL HOLMES JR.

There is one thing stronger than all the armies of the world—and that is an idea whose time has come.
— VICTOR HUGO

Introducing ideas is like introducing new friends. It takes time to know and understand people before someone else's friends become our friends as well. Therefore, when you introduce new ideas to someone else, you must give them sufficient time to get to know them before you can expect agreement.
— CHESTER KARRAS

If we watch ourselves honestly, we shall often find that we have begun to argue against a new idea even before it has been completely stated.
— ARTHUR KOESTLER

Any idea which is six years ahead of its time is a bad idea.
— GEORGE LOIS

The human mind treats a new idea the way a body treats a strange protein; it rejects it.
— PETER MEDAWAR

When an idea is being pushed because it is "exciting," "new," or "innovative"—beware. An exciting, new, innovative idea can also be foolish. — DONALD RUMSFELD

When an idea is too weak to stand the test of simple expression, it should be dropped. — MARQUIS DE VAUVENARGUES

Very few are able to raise themselves above the ideas of the times. — VOLTAIRE

Ideas won't keep. Something must be done about them. When the idea is new, its custodians have fervor, live for it, and, if need be, die for it. — ALFRED NORTH WHITEHEAD

If an idea cannot be expressed in terms of people, it is a sure sign it is irrelevant to the real problems of life.
— COLIN WILSON

See also Vision

INDIVIDUALITY

A man who wants to lead the orchestra must turn his back on the crowd. — JAMES CROOK

To be nobody-but-yourself in a world which is doing its best, night and day, to make you everybody-else means to fight the hardest battle which any human being can fight, and never stop fighting. — E E CUMMINGS

Nature never rhymes her children, nor makes two men alike.
— RALPH WALDO EMERSON

No member of a crew is praised for the rugged individuality of his rowing.
— RALPH WALDO EMERSON

Do not wish to be anything but what you are, and try to be that perfectly.
— SAINT FRANCIS DE SALES

As regards intellectual work, it remains a fact, indeed, that great decisions in the realms of thought and momentous discoveries and solutions of problems are only possible to an individual, working in solitude.
— SIGMUND FREUD

Originality exists in every individual because each of us differs from the others. We are all primary numbers divisible only by ourselves.
— JEAN GUITTON

The strongest man in the world is he who stands alone.
— HENRIK IBSEN

No man ever yet became great by imitation.
— SAMUEL JOHNSON

Eccentricity has always abounded when and where strength of character has abounded. . . . That so few dare to be eccentric marks the chief danger of the time.
— JOHN STUART MILL

You shall know the truth and the truth shall make you odd.
— FLANNERY O'CONNOR

Inside my empty bottle I was constructing a lighthouse while all the others were making ships.
— CHARLES SIMIC

INDIVIDUALITY

If a man does not keep pace with his companions, perhaps it is because he hears a different drummer. Let him step to the music which he hears, however measured or far away.

— HENRY DAVID THOREAU

See also Integrity and Reputation

INITIATIVE

He who chooses to sleep when the house burns may sleep forever.

— AFRICAN PROVERB

Even if you are on the right track, you'll get run over if you just sit there.

— JAMES BALDWIN

Nobody made a greater mistake than he who did nothing because he could do only a little.

— EDMUND BURKE

Everyone who's ever taken a shower has had an idea. It's the person who gets out of the shower, dries off, and does something about it who makes a difference.

— NOLAN BUSHNELL

If a thing is worth doing, it is worth doing badly.

— G. K. CHESTERTON

The path of duty lies in the thing nearby, but men seek it in things far off.

— CHINESE PROVERB

Everything comes to him who hustles while he waits.

— THOMAS EDISON

When the snake is in the house, there is no need to discuss the matter at length.

— EVVE PROVERB, GHANA

Diligence is the mother of good luck.

— BENJAMIN FRANKLIN

It's amazing what you can get done when you don't mind who gets the credit.

— BENJAMIN FRANKLIN

The winds and waves are always on the side of the ablest navigators.

— EDWARD GIBBON

[They] did nothing in particular,
And did it very well.

— W. S. GILBERT

You must get involved to have an impact. No one is impressed with the won-lost record of the referee.

— JOHN H. HOLCOMB

Nothing will ever be attempted, if all possible objections must be first overcome.

— SAMUEL JOHNSON

Those that have done nothing in life are not qualified to judge those that have done little.

— SAMUEL JOHNSON

Nothing could be done at all if a man waited till he could do it so well that no one could find fault with it.

— CARDINAL NEWMAN

When there's no wind, row.

— POLISH PROVERB

But above all try something.

— FRANKLIN D. ROOSEVELT

Do what you can, with what you have, where you are.

— THEODORE ROOSEVELT

Resting isn't getting there.

— UGANDAN PROVERB

Changing one thing for the better is worth more than proving a thousand things are wrong.

— UNKNOWN

Initiative is doing the right thing without being ordered to do it.

— UNKNOWN

You can never get much done unless you go ahead and do it before you are ready.

— UNKNOWN

Do not let what you cannot do interfere with what you can do.

— JOHN WOODEN

See also Action; Change; Effort and Work; Priorities

INTEGRITY AND REPUTATION

Care for the truth more than what people think.

— ARISTOTLE

Expedients are for the hour; principles for the ages.

— HENRY WARD BEECHER

A person of integrity is one who has established a system of values against which all of life is judged.

— V. GILBERT BEERS

A good name is more desirable than great riches; to be esteemed is better than silver or gold.

— THE BIBLE, PROVERBS 22:1

Integrity has no need of rules.

— ALBERT CAMUS

Integrity entails not only a discernment of the right action but a willingness to act on one's conclusions.   — STEPHEN L. CARTER

Any dead thing can go with the stream; it takes something alive to swim against it.   — G. K. CHESTERTON

There are two modes of establishing our reputation: to be praised by honest men, and to be abused by rogues.

— CHARLES CALEB COLTON

The superior man understands what is right; the inferior man understands what will sell.   — CONFUCIUS

To see what is right, and not do it, is want of courage, or of principle.   — CONFUCIUS

The important thing is to be able at any moment to sacrifice what we are for what we could become.   — CHARLES DU BOIS

Once you give up integrity, the rest is a piece of cake.

— J. R. EWING, FROM THE TV SERIES *DALLAS*

You must be able to go into any room anywhere in the world and know there'll be no one there who can point a finger at you and say, "That man did me down."   — LORD FORTE

If you get a reputation for being honest, you have 95 percent of the competition already beat. — JOHN KENNETH GALBRAITH

Nothing is more surely stabilizing than confidence that the leader is unshakably fair in private as well as in public.
— JOHN W. GARDNER

Never, "for the sake of peace and quiet," deny your own experience and convictions. — DAG HAMMARSKJÖLD

Once we assuage our conscience by calling something a "necessary evil," it begins to look more and more necessary and less and less evil. — SYDNEY J. HARRIS

A leader is asking for the trust of people. A leader has to have impeccable integrity, because there is a bond almost like that between a doctor and a patient. People are putting their faith in someone, and in return there must be impeccable integrity. There has to be a sense that leaders are dealing straight, that they are leveling with people. . . . I would say that integrity in a very focused way is number one. — BERNADINE HEALY

I cannot and will not cut my conscience to fit this year's fashions. — LILLIAN HELLMAN

He who trims himself to suit everybody will soon whittle himself away. — R. HULL

Nobody can acquire honor by doing what is wrong.
— THOMAS JEFFERSON

Integrity is keeping my commitment even if the circumstances when I made the commitment have changed.
— DAVID JEREMIAH

Integrity without knowledge is weak and useless, and knowledge without integrity is dangerous and dreadful.

— SAMUEL JOHNSON

The notion that nice guys finish last is not only poisonous but wrong. In fact, the contrary is true. Unethical conduct is always self-destructive and generates more unethical conduct until you hit the pits. The challenge is not always being ethical and paying a big price. The challenge is to be ethical and get what you want. I think you can do it almost every time.

— MICHAEL JOSEPHSON

Act only on that maxim whereby you can at the same time will that it should become a universal law.   — IMMANUEL KANT

The time is always right to do what is right.

— MARTIN LUTHER KING JR.

There is always the danger that we will permit the means by which we live to replace the ends for which we live.

— MARTIN LUTHER KING JR.

A leader with integrity has one self, at home and at work, with family and with colleagues. He or she has a unifying set of values that guide choices of action regardless of the situation.

— JAMES KOUZES AND BARRY POSNER

It's a matter of having principles. It's easy to have principles when you're rich. The important thing is to have principles when you're poor.   — RAY KROC

I desire so to conduct the affairs of this administration that if at the end, when I come to lay down the reins of power, I have lost every friend on earth, I shall at least have one friend left, and that friend shall be down inside me. — ABRAHAM LINCOLN

Do the truth you know, and you shall learn the truth you need to know. — GEORGE MACDONALD

To be trusted is a greater compliment than to be loved. — GEORGE MACDONALD

I can honestly say that I was never affected by the question of the success of an undertaking. If I felt it was the right thing to do, I was for it regardless of the possible outcome. — GOLDA MEIR

People think that if they avoid the truth, it might change to something better before they have to hear it. — MARSHA NORMAN

Right is right, even if everyone is against it; and wrong is wrong, even if everyone is for it. — WILLIAM PENN

There is no such thing as a minor lapse of integrity. — TOM PETERS

Learn what you are, and be such. — PINDAR

Integrity is so perishable in the summer months of success. — VANESSA REDGRAVE

Conscience warns us as a friend before it punishes as a judge. — STANISLAS I, KING OF POLAND

You should not live one way in private, another in public.

— PUBLILIUS SYRUS

Blessed is he whose fame does not outshine his truth.

— RABINDRANATH TAGORE

Few men have the virtue to withstand the highest bidder.

— GEORGE WASHINGTON

See also Character

INTUITION AND INSTINCTS

Wayne Gretzky, the best hockey player of his generation, said that it's not as important to know where the puck is now as to know where it will be. Leaders have the sense of where the culture is going to be, where the organization must be if it is to grow.

— WARREN BENNIS

Never use intuition.

— OMAR BRADLEY

Trust your hunches. They're usually based on facts filed away just below the conscious level.

— JOYCE BROTHERS

The only really valuable thing is intuition.

— ALBERT EINSTEIN

Trust your heart. . . . Never deny it a hearing. It is the kind of house oracle that often foretells the most important.

— BALTASAR GRACIÁN

Intuition—the supra-logic that cuts out all routine processes of thought and leaps straight from problem to answer.

— ROBERT GRAVES

The more faithfully you listen to the voice within you, the better you will hear what is sounding outside.

— DAG HAMMARSKJÖLD

A moment's insight is sometimes worth a life's experience.

— OLIVER WENDALL HOLMES SR.

Wait for your cues, and give them your full attention.

— YALE KNEELAND

How can you develop your intuitive powers? Like any other form of thinking, intuition requires an alertness, sensitivity and discipline of mind which have to be cultivated. . . . Intuition isn't the enemy, but the ally, of reason.

— JOHN KORD LAGEMANN

Intuition becomes increasingly valuable in the new information society precisely because there is so much data.

— JOHN NAISBITT

The final act of business judgment is intuitive.

— UNKNOWN

The problem with insight, sensitivity and intuition is that they tend to confirm our biases.   — NAOMI WEISSTEIN

See also Creativity; Problems and Problem Solving

JUDGMENT

A reputation for good judgment, for fair dealing, for truth, and for rectitude, is itself a fortune. — HENRY WARD BEECHER

Life is the art of drawing sufficient conclusions from insufficient premises. — SAMUEL BUTLER

Let us keep our mouths shut and our pens dry until we know the facts. — A. J. CARLSON

True genius resides in the capacity for evaluation of uncertain, hazardous, and conflicting information. — WINSTON CHURCHILL

Statistics are no substitute for judgment. — HENRY CLAY

Learning is not wisdom; information does not guarantee good judgment. — JOHN DEWEY

Our duty is to believe that for which we have sufficient evidence, and to suspend our judgment when we have not. — JOHN LUBBOCK

The acid test of an officer who aspires to high command is his ability to be able to grasp quickly the essentials of a military problem, to decide rapidly what he will do, to make it quite clear to all concerned what he intends to achieve and how he will do it, and then to see that his subordinate commanders get on with the job. — BERNARD L. MONTGOMERY

Often a dash of judgment is better than a flash of genius. — HOWARD W. NEWTON

A good general not only sees the way to victory; he also knows when victory is impossible. — POLYBIUS

You are given a situation. What you are determines what you see; what you see determines what you do.

— HADDON ROBINSON

You gotta know when to hold 'em, and know when to fold 'em. — KENNY ROGERS' SONG, "THE GAMBLER"

To judge a thing, one must first know the standard.

— SANSKRIT PROVERB

Intelligence is quickness in seeing things as they are.

— GEORGE SANTAYANA

Any fool can keep a rule. God gave him a brain to know when to break the rule. — WILLARD W. SCOTT JR.

A man's judgment is best when he can forget himself and any reputation he may have acquired and can concentrate wholly on making the right decisions. — RAYMOND A. SPRUANCE

Always "err," as God does, on the side of freedom, mercy and compassion. — PHILIP YANCEY

See also Wisdom

LEADERSHIP — CHARACTERISTICS AND QUALITIES

He who has never learned to obey cannot be a good commander.
— ARISTOTLE

The art of leadership is saying no, not yes. It is very easy to say yes.
— TONY BLAIR

The heart of a statesman must be in his head.
— NAPOLEON BONAPARTE

A leader is a dealer in hope.
— NAPOLEON BONAPARTE

A leader of men must make decisions quickly; be independent; act and stand firm; be a fighter; speak openly, plainly, frankly; make defeats his lessons; cooperate; coordinate; use the best of any alliances or allies; walk with active faith courageously toward danger or the unknown; create a staff; know, love, and represent the best interests of his followers; be loyal, true, frank, and faithful; reward loyalty; have a high, intelligent, and worthy purpose and ideal. Do justice; love mercy; fear no man but fear only God.
— JOHN W. DODGE

Leadership always has three basic requirements: a leader, follower(s), and a situation. These elements are as essential to leadership as oxygen, fuel, and heat are to fire. If any one is removed, leadership will disappear—the fire will go out.
— E. J. ELLISTON

Ninety percent of leadership is the ability to communicate something people want.
— DIANE FEINSTEIN

Leadership is heading into the wind with such knowledge of oneself and such collaborative energy as to move others to wish to follow. The angle into the wind is less important than choosing one and sticking reasonably to it, which reasonability includes willingness to be borne by friendly currents.

— THEODORE FRIEND III

All of the great leaders have had one characteristic in common: it was the willingness to confront unequivocally the major anxiety of their people in their time. This, and not much else, is the essence of leadership.

— JOHN KENNETH GALBRAITH

Leadership cannot really be taught. It can only be learned.

— HAROLD GENEEN

One of the tests of leadership is the ability to recognize a problem before it becomes an emergency.

— ARNOLD H. GLASGOW

Faith in the ability of a leader is of slight service unless it be united with faith in his justice.   — GEORGE W. GOETHALS

Leadership is one of the things you cannot delegate. You either exercise it, or you abdicate it.   — ROBERT GOIZUETA

Leaders need "a sense for the unknowable" and the ability to "foresee the unforeseeable."   — ROBERT GREENLEAF

A statesman should follow public opinion as a coachman follows his horses: having firm hold on the reins, and guiding them.   — J. C. HARE

Good leaders resemble each other but each bad leader is bad in his own way, just as there is only one kind of good health but many kinds of sickness. — ANTHONY JAY

There are basically two kinds of leaders: those who sacrifice the people for themselves, and those who sacrifice themselves for the people. — RICK JOYNER

Leadership and learning are indispensable to each other.
— JOHN F. KENNEDY

He who walks far in advance of his contemporaries is a leader, even though centuries may pass before he is recognized as such and intelligently followed. — IBN KHALDUN

The difference between great and ordinary leaders is less formal intellect than insight and courage. The great man understands the essence of a problem; the ordinary leader grasps only the symptoms. The great man focuses on the relationship of events to each other; the ordinary man sees only a series of seemingly disconnected events. The great man has a vision of the future that enables him to put obstacles in perspective; the ordinary leader turns pebbles in the road into boulders. — HENRY KISSINGER

Wanting to lead and believing that you can lead are only the departure points on the path to leadership. Leadership is an art, a performing art. And in the art of leadership, the artist's instrument is the self. The mastery of the art of leadership comes with the mastery of the self. Ultimately, leadership development is a process of self-development.
— JAMES KOUZES AND BARRY POSNER

As for the best leaders, the people do not notice their existence. The next best, the people honor and praise. The next, the people fear; and the next, the people hate. . . . When the best leader's work is done the people say, "We did it ourselves." — LAO-TZU

Leaders don't force people to follow; they invite them on a journey. — CHARLES S. LAUER

There are many kinds of leaders. Some are natural leaders, "born leaders," having the personality and skill that equip them for the role and responsibilities of leadership. Others have learned how to be leaders. They have read, studied, practiced. To them, the gift of leadership is a capacity to be honed and perfected; it is a learned art, not a natural skill. They are made, not born. — HARRIS LEE

The final test of a leader is that he leaves behind him in other men the conviction and the will to carry on.
— WALTER LIPPMANN

The most important quality in a leader is that of being acknowledged as such. — ANDRÉ MAUROIS

The leader understands that sustained long-term results cannot be achieved by pushing people to do things. He attracts followers in much the same way as a magnet attracts particles of metal. — DALE McCONKEY

Loyalty is the greatest characteristic trait needed in an executive. — CHARLES P. McCORMICK

Leadership is action, not position.
— DONALD H. McGANNON

The real leader has no need to lead—he is content to point the way. — HENRY MILLER

The leader must have infectious optimism. . . . The final test of a leader is the feeling you have when you leave his presence after a conference. Have you a feeling of uplift and confidence? — BERNARD L. MONTGOMERY

Leadership means having the courage to take decisions, not for easy headlines in ten days but for a better country in ten years. — BRIAN MULRONEY

Blindness in a leader is unpardonable.

— JAWAHARLAL NEHRU

The best leaders are apt to be found among those executives who have a strong component of unorthodoxy in their characters. Instead of resisting innovation, they embrace it.

— DAVID OGILVY

The captain of a ship is not chosen from those of the passengers who come from the best family. — BLAISE PASCAL

Eagles don't flock—you have to find them one at a time.

— H. ROSS PEROT

Executive ability is deciding quickly and getting somebody else to do the work. — J. G. POLLARD

You have achieved excellence as a leader when people will follow you everywhere if only out of curiosity. — COLIN POWELL

A leader is a person who, while being awake, wakes up a bit more. — ROBERT RABBIN

The philosophy of life is the foundation stone of your leadership. — HAL REED

A leader has two important characteristics: first, he is going somewhere; second, he is able to persuade other people to go with him. — MAXIMILIEN FRANÇOIS DE ROBESPIERRE

A leader needs to be one of us—a commoner—and, at the same time, better than us—a king. — WILLIAM P. ROBINSON

Leadership, . . . as someone once observed, is like the abominable snowman: you see the tracks but never the thing itself. — ROGER B. SMITH

The shepherd always tries to persuade the sheep that their interests and his own are the same. — STENDHAL

A man was chief only as long as he did the will of the people. If he got to be too chiefy, he'd go to sleep one night, and wake up the next morning to find that he was chief all to himself. The tribe would move away in the night, and they didn't wait four years to do it either. — SUN BEAR

Weak leadership can wreck the soundest strategy; forceful execution of even a poor plan can often bring victory.
— SUN ZI

A good leader inspires others with confidence in him; a great leader inspires them with confidence in themselves.
— UNKNOWN

Only he deserves to lead who just as soon would not.
— UNKNOWN

One of the things about leadership is that you cannot be a moderate, balanced, thoughtful, careful articulator of policy. You've got to be on the lunatic fringe. — JACK WELCH

I don't base my actions on popularity. If you're in a position of leadership, you can't wait to determine how it's going to affect you in terms of good or bad. You have to lead and do what you think is good. — DOUGLAS WILDER

The ear of the leader must ring with the voices of the people. — WOODROW WILSON

The most self-conscious people in the world are its leaders. They may also be the most anxious and insecure. As men of action, leaders face risks and uncertainty, and often display remarkable courage in shouldering grave responsibility. But beneath their fortitude, there often lies an agonizing sense of doubt and a need to justify themselves. — ABRAHAM ZALEZNIK

LEADERSHIP DEFINED

There are almost as many different definitions of leadership as there are persons who have attempted to define the concept. — BERNARD BASS

Leadership . . . involves revealing to others a purpose as yet unrecognized, elevating a present goal given too low a priority, or exposing a threat that is perceived but not fully understood. — JACK N. BEHRMAN

Leadership is the capacity to translate vision into reality. — WARREN BENNIS

Managers are people who do things right, and leaders are people who do the right things. — WARREN BENNIS

The ultimate test of practical leadership is the realization of intended, real change that meets people's enduring needs.
— JAMES MACGREGOR BURNS

Management is efficiency in climbing the ladder of success; leadership determines whether the ladder is leaning against the right wall. — STEPHEN R. COVEY

Leadership is liberating people to do what is required of them in the most effective and the most human way possible.
— MAX DEPREE

Leadership is lifting a person's vision to higher sights, the raising of a person's performance to a higher standard, the building of a personality beyond its normal limitations.
— PETER DRUCKER

Leadership is the art of getting someone else to do something you want done because he wants to do it.
— DWIGHT D. EISENHOWER

In the simplest terms, a leader is one who knows where he wants to go, and gets up and goes. — JOHN ERSKINE

Leadership is the special quality which enables people to stand up and pull the rest of us over the horizon. — JAMES L. FISHER

Leadership is the priceless gift that you earn from the people who work for you. I have to earn the right to that gift and have to continuously re-earn that right. — JOHN HARVEY-JONES

You can judge a leader by the size of the problems he tackles —people nearly always pick a problem their own size, and ignore or leave others the bigger or smaller ones.

— ANTHONY JAY

A leader: An individual who created an alchemy of vision that moved people from where they were to places that they have never been before.   — HENRY KISSINGER

Leadership is the use of power. But power, to be ethical, must never be abused. To ensure that, one rule cannot be broken: Power is to be used only for the benefit of others, never for yourself. That is the essential generosity and self-sacrifice of the leader.   — PETER KOESTENBAUM

Leadership is disciplined passion.

— JAMES KOUZES AND BARRY POSNER

Leadership is influence.

— JOHN C. MAXWELL

Leadership may be defined as that quality in a leader that inspires sufficient confidence in his subordinates as to be willing to accept his views and carry out his commands.

— CHESTER NIMITZ

Leadership appears to be the art of getting others to want to do something you are convinced should be done.

— VANCE PACKARD

Leadership is the art of accomplishing more than the science of management says is possible.   — COLIN POWELL

Leadership is the transference of vision.

— HAL REED

Good leadership consists in showing average people how to do the work of superior people. — JOHN D. ROCKEFELLER

LEADERSHIP — ITS DIFFICULTIES AND DEMANDS

Trying to make the presidency work these days is like trying to sew buttons on a custard pie. — JAMES DAVID BARBER

Learning leadership is like learning to play the violin in public. — WARREN BENNIS AND BURT NANUS

When you become a leader, you lose the right to think about yourself. — GERALD BROOKS

What the president of the United States, the president of a major company or a consulting firm, and the president of a college or university have in common is that they all must lead in an environment where consensus is the exception, not the norm. — MADELEINE F. GREEN

Administrators cannot be given the responsibilities of statesmen without likewise incurring the tribulations of politicians. — PENDLETON HERRING

Beware of the chief seat, because it shifts.

— JEWISH PROVERB

Life always gets harder toward the summit — the cold increases, responsibility increases. — FRIEDRICH NIETZSCHE

A leader who keeps his ear to the ground allows his rear end to become a target.
— ANGIE PAPADAKIS

Uneasy lies the head that wears a crown.
— WILLIAM SHAKESPEARE, HENRY IV, PART 2

LEADERSHIP — FINISHING WELL

Leaders who finish well are not those who run the last race before the track lights are turned off. Leaders who finish well are those who pass the baton to their successors to run the next leg of the race. Blessed are those who make their successors succeed.
— LEITH ANDERSON

A great man leaves clean work behind him and requires no sweeper up of the chips.
— ELIZABETH BARRETT BROWNING

From a management point of view, Shakespeare's King Lear is a tragedy because Lear failed to understand two managerial precepts: the need to select competent successors, and the need to let go.
— JOHN K. CLEMENS AND DOUGLAS F. MAYER

Next to the assumption of power is the responsibility of relinquishing it.
— BENJAMIN DISRAELI

There's a trick to the Graceful Exit. It begins with the vision to recognize when a job, a life stage, a relationship is over — and let it go. . . . It involves a sense of future, a belief that every exit line is an entry, that we are moving on, rather than out.
— ELLEN GOODMAN

When leaders have fulfilled their functions, it's time for them to retire. — NATHAN HARE

Few men of action have been able to make a graceful exit at the appropriate time. — MALCOLM MUGGERIDGE

All ballplayers should quit when it starts to feel as if all the baselines run uphill. — BABE RUTH

Leaders should lead as far as they can and then vanish. Their ashes should not choke the fire they have lit. — H. G. WELLS

There is a time for departure even when there's no certain place to go. — TENNESSEE WILLIAMS

The completion of an important project has every right to be dignified by a natural grieving process. Something that required the best of us has ended. We will miss it.
— ANNE WILSON-SCHAEF

LEADERSHIP — MISCELLANEOUS

Great necessities call forth great leaders.
— ABIGAIL ADAMS

There are no bad regiments, only bad colonels.
— NAPOLEON BONAPARTE

Divorced from ethics, leadership is reduced to management and politics to mere technique. — JAMES MACGREGOR BURNS

Leadership is one of the most observed and least understood phenomena on earth. — JAMES MACGREGOR BURNS

An army of a thousand is easy to find, but, ah, how difficult to find a general. — CHINESE PROVERB

It is better to have a lion at the head of an army of sheep, than a sheep at the head of an army of lions. — DANIEL DEFOE

Loyalty is the one thing a leader cannot do without. — A. P. GOUTHEY

Leaders are always failing somebody. — RONALD A. HEIFETZ

Do not walk through time without leaving worthy evidence of your passage. — POPE JOHN XXIII

Have you ever noticed how often people use "battle" images as they go about the work of leadership? We talk about "do or die" tactics and strategy, about using our big guns, about allies and enemies, about wins and losses. The imagery suggests that if we fail to be fiercely competitive, we will lose, because the basic structure of the universe is a vast combat zone. The tragedy of that inner shadow, that unexamined inner fear of failing, is that it helps create situations where people actually have to live that way. — PARKER J. PALMER

The actions of those who hold great power, and pass their lives in a lofty status, are known to all men. Therefore, in the highest position there is the least freedom of action. — SALLUST

In calm water, every ship has a good captain. — SWEDISH PROVERB

Consensus is the negation of leadership.

— Margaret Thatcher

I sit here all day trying to persuade people to do the things they ought to have sense enough to do without my persuading them. That's all the powers of the president amount to.

— Harry S. Truman

Either lead, follow or get out of the way.

— Unknown

The future will not belong to managers or to those who make the numbers dance, or to those who are conversant with all the jargon we use to sound smart. The world will belong to passionate, driven leaders — people who not only have an enormous energy, but who can energize those whom they lead.

— Jack Welch

Whether a man is burdened by power or enjoys power; whether he is trapped by responsibility or made free by it; whether he is moved by other people and outer forces or moves them — this is of the essence of leadership.

— Theodore H. White

LEADERSHIP — TASKS AND DUTIES

Becoming a manager has much to do with learning the metaphors; becoming a good manager has much to do with using the metaphors; and becoming a leader has much to do with changing the metaphors.

— Jim Autry

The ruler over a country of a thousand chariots must give diligent attention to business; he must be sincere; he must be economical; he must love his people; and he must provide employment for them at the proper seasons. — CONFUCIUS

A leader must recognize that, in the end, there are worse things even than defeat. When facts dictate that one's business has failed, or that one's war is lost, and that no further effort could possibly achieve success, a leader knows it is far better to face facts squarely than to carry on a struggle that results only in needless effusions of red ink or red blood, or reputations or lives destroyed. Ultimately, a leader must count the costs of sacrifice not only to himself but to his people and act accordingly. — H. W. CROCKER

I am not supposed to be an expert in every field. I am supposed to be an expert in picking experts. — MOSHE DAYAN

Delegate everything but final authority.
— JAMES L. FISHER

One could argue that willingness to engage in battle when necessary is a *sine qua non* of leadership. — JOHN W. GARDNER

Leadership is achieved by ability, alertness, experience; by willingness to accept responsibility; by a knack for getting along with people; by an open mind and a head that stays clear under stress. — E. F. GIRARD

Leadership has a harder job to do than just choose sides. It must bring sides together. — JESSE JACKSON

A president's hardest task is not to do what is right, but to know what is right. — LYNDON B. JOHNSON

They don't make plans; they don't solve problems; they don't even organize people. What leaders really do is prepare organizations for change and help them cope as they struggle through it. — JOHN KOTTER

Leaders who can analyze discord, find some common interests, and persuade each discordant group that its interests lie in pursuing a new set of goals will often take their places in history as the great political figures of their times.

— CHARLES LINDBLOM

I start with the premise that the function of leadership is to produce more leaders, not more followers. — RALPH NADER

If managers are known for their skills in solving problems, then leaders are known for being masters in designing and building institutions; they are the architects of the organization's future. — BURT NANUS

The most effective leader is the one who satisfies the psychological needs of his followers. — DAVID OGILVY

The leader must know, must know that he knows, and must be able to make it abundantly clear to those about him that he knows. — CLARENCE B. RANDALL

Leaders are the ones who keep faith with the past, keep step with the present, and keep the promise to posterity.

— HAROLD J. SEYMOUR

We want all our leaders . . . to stir our souls a little.

— THOMAS TEAL

Some citizens are so good that nothing a leader can do will make them better. Others are so incorrigible that nothing can be done to improve them. But the great bulk of the people go with the moral tide of the moment. The leader must help create that tide.

— Unknown nineteenth century Japanese philosopher

A leader's goal should be to make himself redundant.

— Simon Walker

Now there are five matters to which a general must pay strict heed. The first of these is administration; the second, preparedness; the third, determination; the fourth, prudence; and the fifth, economy.

— Wu Ch'i

MEDIA RELATIONS

Televisio ergo sum—I am televised, therefore I am.

— Russell Baker

Four hostile newspapers are more to be feared than a thousand bayonets.

— Napoleon Bonaparte

Nothing is "really" real unless it happens on television.

— Daniel J. Boorstin

Twenty-five years in Washington has taught me never to tell a lie to a reporter.

— Joseph A. Califano Jr.

"No comment" is a splendid expression. I am using it again and again.

— Winston Churchill

Never know a public man well enough that he inhibits you from writing about him frankly and fully while he's living his public life. — ALISTAIR COOKE

If you want something to remain off the record, don't say it. — ANITA CREAMER

When you're talking to the media, be a well, not a fountain. — MICHAEL DEAVER

If you've got some news that you don't want noticed, put it out Friday afternoon at 4 p.m. — DAVID GERGEN

In the age of television, image becomes more important than substance. — S. I. HAYAKAWA

I want the truth; *they* want to be beautiful. — THOMAS MORGAN, REPORTER

Looking at yourself through the media is like looking at one of those rippled mirrors in an amusement park. — EDMUND S. MUSKIE

Nobody believes the official spokesman but everybody trusts an unidentified source. — RON NESSEN

The American people don't believe anything until they see it on television. — RICHARD M. NIXON

The media are far more powerful than the president in creating public awareness and shaping public opinion, for the simple reason that the media always have the last word. — RICHARD M. NIXON

In dealing with the press, do yourself a favor; stick with one of three responses: (a) I know and I can tell you; (b) I know and I can't tell you; (c) I don't know. — DAN RATHER

There is nothing so small that it can't be blown out of proportion. — RUCHERT'S LAW

Don't do or say things you would not like to see on the front page of the *Washington Post*. — DONALD RUMSFELD

Report me and my cause aright. — WILLIAM SHAKESPEARE, *HAMLET*

It is better to appear in hell than in the newspapers. — SPANISH PROVERB

For those who govern, the first thing required is indifference to newspapers. — LOUIS ADOLPHE THIERS

He who is created by television can be destroyed by television. — THEODORE H. WHITE

When a reporter sits down at the typewriter, he's nobody's friend. — THEODORE H. WHITE

Journalists are not your friends. It's not that reporters aren't decent people—they are. They are not interviewing you to meet a new friend, but to get a story. Their job always comes first and don't forget it. — ROBERT L. WOODRUM

See also Communication

MENTORING

Example is the school of mankind; they will learn at no other.
— EDMUND BURKE

Mentoring is a brain to pick, a shoulder to cry on, and a kick in the pants.
— JOHN C. CROSBY

The greatest good you can do for another is not just to share your riches but to reveal to him his own.
— BENJAMIN DISRAELI

Our chief want in life is somebody who shall make us what we can be.
— RALPH WALDO EMERSON

The growth and development of people is the highest calling of leadership.
— HARVEY S. FIRESTONE

Mentor: Someone who helps another person become what that person aspires to be.
— M. S. GLADSTONE

If I accept you as you are, I will make you worse; however, if I treat you as though you are what you are capable of becoming, I help you become that.
— JOHANN WOLFGANG VON GOETHE

People seldom improve when they have no model but themselves to copy after.
— OLIVER GOLDSMITH

Nothing is so infectious as example.
— CHARLES KINGSLEY

A strong leader knows that if he develops his associates he will be even stronger.
— JAMES F. LINCOLN

Good mentorship . . . is based on honesty. Good mentors give you bad news, and then help you grow out of it; they give you good news and help you see beyond it. — TED MITCHELL

The first great gift we can bestow on others is a good example. — FREDERIC MORELL

[G]ood mentors help to anchor the promise of the future. — SHARON DALOZ PARKS

Mentors dance an intricate two-step, because they practice the art of supporting and challenging more or less simultaneously. While giving the well-timed push into a new area of potential competence, the mentor may also provide counsel when a protégé is in well over his head. — SHARON DALOZ PARKS

The best way to really train people is with an experienced mentor . . . and on the job. — TOM PETERS

Finding and making use of the right mentor is the most critical step you'll ever take in your career. — LINDA PHILLIPS-JONES

Example is not the main thing in influencing others. It is the only thing. — ALBERT SCHWEITZER

Perhaps the most profound thing about being a mentor is that, for the most part, you don't know you are one until somebody tells you. — SALLY WEBER

See also People Skills; Talent

MISCELLANEOUS ADVICE AND INSIGHTS

Growth for the sake of growth is the ideology of the cancer cell.
— EDWARD ABBEY

Resist your time—take a foothold outside it.
— LORD ACTON

Every ruler is harsh whose rule is new.
— AESCHYLUS

It is better to abolish serfdom from above than to wait for it to abolish itself from below.
— ALEXANDER II

Observe your enemies, for they first find out your faults.
— ANTISTHENES

Leaders value learning and mastery, and so do people who work for leaders. Leaders make it clear that there is no failure, only mistakes that give us feedback and tell us what to do next.
— WARREN BENNIS

We have this fantasy that if we just have enough information, we can control events.
— BARBARA BIESECKER

Always make yourself essential; that's been my golden rule.
— JOH BJELKE-PETERSEN

It is our relation to circumstances that determines their influence over us. The same wind that carries one vessel into port may blow another off shore.
— CHRISTIAN NESTELL BOVEE

You lean a little to the left and then a little to the right in order to always move straight ahead.
— JERRY BROWN, LIKENING THE ART OF GOVERNMENT TO PADDLING A CANOE

Learning is rowing upstream; advance or lose all.
— CHINESE PROVERB

I am an optimist. It does not seem too much use being anything else.
— WINSTON CHURCHILL (ALSO ATTRIBUTED TO OTHERS)

An organization does well only those things the boss checks.
— BRUCE C. CLARKE

Never try to teach a pig to sing; it wastes your time and it annoys the pig.
— PAUL DICKSON

I am a man of fixed and unbending principles, the first of which is to be flexible at all times.
— EVERETT M. DIRKSEN

Do not believe that it is very much of an advance to do the unnecessary three times as fast.
— PETER DRUCKER

Make strengths productive, weaknesses irrelevant.
— PETER DRUCKER

History teaches us that men and nations behave wisely once they have exhausted all other alternatives.
— ABBA EBAN

Good men prefer to be accountable.
— MICHAEL EDWARDES

Administrative subordinates either agree with the president, change the president's mind, or resign.
— JAMES L. FISHER

You cannot shake hands with a clenched fist.

— Indira Gandhi

There is nothing more frightening than ignorance in action.

— Johann Wolfgang von Goethe

Reason may be the lever, but sentiment gives you the fulcrum and the place to stand on if you want to move the world.

— Oliver Wendell Holmes Sr.

Lots of folks confuse bad management with destiny.

— Elbert Hubbard

See everything, overlook a lot, correct a little.

— Pope John XXIII

Some people are so busy learning the tricks of the trade that they never learn the trade.

— Vernon Law

The only people who achieve much are those who want knowledge so badly that they seek it while the conditions are still unfavorable. Favorable conditions never come.

— C. S. Lewis

I have always found that mercy bears richer fruits than strict justice.

— Abraham Lincoln

No quarrel ought ever to be converted into a policy.

— David Lloyd George

Organizing is what you do before you do something, so that when you do it, it's not all mixed up.

— A. A. Milne

Stubborn opposition to proposals often has no other basis than the complaining question, "Why wasn't I consulted?"

— DANIEL PATRICK MOYNIHAN

Confidence is contagious. So is lack of confidence.

— MICHAEL O'BRIEN

The secret of business is to know something that nobody else knows.

— ARISTOTLE ONASSIS

Don't fight a battle if you don't gain anything by winning.

— GEORGE S. PATTON

Issuing orders is worth about 10 percent. The remaining 90 percent consists in assuring proper and vigorous execution of the order.

— GEORGE S. PATTON

Luck and strength go together. When you get lucky, you have to have the strength to follow through. You also have to have the strength to wait for the luck.

— MARIO PUZO

The person who knows "how" will always have a job. The person who knows "why" will always be his boss.

— DIANE RAVITCH

Men who are weak never give in when they should.

— CARDINAL DE RETZ

Do not hit at all if it can be avoided, but never hit softly.

— THEODORE ROOSEVELT

Be able to resign. It will improve your value to the president and do wonders for your performance.

— DONALD RUMSFELD

Be not afraid of greatness: some are born great, some achieve greatness, and some have greatness thrust upon them.

— WILLIAM SHAKESPEARE, *TWELFTH NIGHT*

Management, like mass transit, is only noticed when it is bad.

— EVERETT T. SUTERS

Worry saps a man's strength.

— THE TALMUD

People mistake their limitations for high standards.

— JEAN TOOMER

Your best hope for success is that your associates aren't as good at judging you as you are at judging them.   — FRANK TYGER

Never scratch a tiger with a short stick.

— UNKNOWN

Politics: the art of making possible that which is necessary.

— PAUL VALÉRY

Great men undertake great things because they are great; fools, because they think them easy.   — MARQUIS DE VAUVENARGUES

It is easier to resist at the beginning than at the end.

— LEONARDO DA VINCI

Seek simplicity and then distrust it.

— ALFRED NORTH WHITEHEAD

Always remember what you're good at and stick with it.

— ERMENEGILDO ZEGNA

Nobody notices when things go right.

— M. ZIMMERMAN

MISTAKES

One CEO told me that if she had a knack for leadership, it was the capacity to make as many mistakes as she could as soon as possible, and thus get them out of the way. Another said that a mistake is simply "another way of doing things." These leaders learn from and use something that doesn't go well; it is not a failure, but simply the next step.

— WARREN BENNIS

Every great mistake has a halfway moment, a split second when it can be recalled and perhaps remedied.

— PEARL S. BUCK

They defend their errors as if they were defending their inheritance.

— EDMUND BURKE

To err is human but only fools go on doing it.

— CICERO

Half of our mistakes in life arise from feeling where we ought to think, and thinking where we ought to feel.

— JOHN CHURTON COLLINS

A man who has committed a mistake and doesn't correct it is committing another mistake.

— CONFUCIUS

I have learned more from my mistakes than from my successes.

— HUMPHREY DAVY

It never bothers me for people to make a mistake if they had a reason for what they did. If they can tell me, "I thought this and reasoned so, and came to that decision," if they obviously went through a reasonable thought process to get where they did, even if it didn't turn out right, that's OK. The ones you want to watch out for are those who can't even tell you why they did what they did. — FRANK GAINES

Freedom is not worth having if it does not include the freedom to make mistakes. — MAHATMA GANDHI

No man ever became great or good except through many and great mistakes. — WILLIAM GLADSTONE

We ought to be able to learn some things second hand. There is not enough time to make all the mistakes ourselves.
— HARRIET HALL

Any man worth his salt will stick up for what he believes right, but it takes a slightly bigger man to acknowledge instantly and without reservation that he is in error.
— PEYTON C. MARCH

It is better to make a mistake with the full force of your being than to carefully avoid mistakes with a trembling spirit. Responsibility means recognizing both pleasure and price, making a choice on that recognition, and then living with that choice without concern. — DAN MILLMAN

We may make mistakes—but they must never be mistakes which result from faintness of heart or abandonment of moral principle. — FRANKLIN D. ROOSEVELT

If you foul up, tell the president and correct it fast. Delay only compounds mistakes. — DONALD RUMSFELD

A life spent making mistakes is not only more honorable but more useful than a life spent doing nothing.
— GEORGE BERNARD SHAW

It doesn't matter how much milk you spill just so long as you don't lose your cow. — TEXAS SAYING

No matter how far you have gone on a wrong road, turn back. — TURKISH PROVERB

If you don't learn from your mistakes there isn't much sense in making them. — UNKNOWN

People will tolerate honest mistakes, but if you violate their trust you will find it very difficult to ever regain their confidence. — CRAIG WEATHERUP

See also Experience; Failure

OPEN-MINDEDNESS

If in the last few years you haven't discarded a major opinion or acquired a new one, check your pulse. You may be dead.
— GELETT BURGESS

An obstinate man does not hold opinions—they hold him.
— JOSEPH BUTLER

If you would convince others, seem open to conviction yourself. — LORD CHESTERFIELD

A closed mind is a dying mind.

— EDNA FERBER

Faced with the choice between changing one's mind and proving there is no need to do so, almost everyone gets busy on the proof. — JOHN KENNETH GALBRAITH

There's something wrong if you're always right.

— ARNOLD H. GLASGOW

Those who never retract their opinions love themselves more than they love the truth. — JOSEPH JOUBERT

Like all weak men he laid an exaggerated stress on not changing one's mind. — W. SOMERSET MAUGHAM

Lord, when I am wrong, make me willing to change; when I am right, make me easy to live with. So strengthen me that the power of my example will far exceed the authority of my rank. — PAULINE H. PETERS

O Lord, grant that we may always be right, for Thou knowest we will never change our minds. — SCOTTISH PRAYER

Nothing undermines openness more surely than certainty. Once we feel as if we have "the answer," all motivation to question our thinking disappears. — PETER SENGE

If there's an opinion, facts will be found to support it.

— JUDY SPROLES

See also Clear Thinking; Values and Beliefs

OPPORTUNITY

In playing ball, or in life, a person occasionally gets the opportunity to do something great. When that time comes, only two things matter: being prepared to seize the moment and having the courage to take your best swing. — HANK AARON

The dawn does not come twice to waken a man.

— ARABIAN PROVERB

When you are an anvil, be patient; when a hammer, strike.

— ARABIAN PROVERB

A wise man will make more opportunities than he finds.

— FRANCIS BACON

Luck? I don't know anything about luck. I've never banked on it, and I'm afraid of people who do. Luck to me is something else: hard work and realizing what is opportunity and what isn't. — LUCILLE BALL

Ability is of little account without opportunity.

— NAPOLEON BONAPARTE

Men stumble over the truth from time to time, but most pick themselves up and hurry off as if nothing happened.

— WINSTON CHURCHILL

Opportunity is sometimes hard to recognize if you're only looking for a lucky break. — MONTA CRANE

Not only strike while the iron is hot, but make it hot by striking.

— OLIVER CROMWELL

Very little time is spent on deliberate thinking or conceptual thinking. There is always a problem to be solved. Problem-solving also implies the removal of risk, whereas opportunity-seeking implies increased risk and work. It is not at all difficult to see why problem-solving is so much preferred to opportunity-seeking. Management is forced to solve problems. No one is forced to look for opportunities until it is too late.   — EDWARD DE BONO

No great man ever complains of want of opportunity.
                                                      — RALPH WALDO EMERSON

Gather ye rosebuds while ye may,
        Old Time is still aflying:
And this same flower that smiles today,
        Tomorrow will be dying.

                                                      — ROBERT HERRICK

Seize the day.
                                                      — HORACE

To improve the golden moment of opportunity, and catch the good that is within our reach, is the great art of life.
                                                      — SAMUEL JOHNSON

Four things come not back: The spoken word; the sped arrow; time past; the neglected opportunity.   — IBN OMAR

Know your opportunity.
                                                      — PITTACUS

Hell is paved with good intentions and roofed with lost opportunities.   — PORTUGUESE PROVERB

I feel that the greatest reward for doing is the opportunity to do more. — Jonas Salk

The opportunity that God sends does not wake up him who sleeps. — Senegalese proverb

There is a tide in the affairs of men, which, taken at the flood, leads on to fortune; omitted, all the voyage of their life is bound in shallows and in miseries; and we must take the current when it serves, or lose our ventures.

— William Shakespeare, *Julius Caesar*

Learn to listen; Opportunity could be knocking at your door very softly. — Frank Tyger

He who hesitates is not only lost, but miles from the next exit.
— Unknown

Luck is where opportunity meets preparation.
— Denzel Washington

See also Preparation

ORGANIZATIONAL STRUCTURES

Intelligent people, when assembled into an organization, will tend toward collective stupidity. — Karl Albrecht

Committee: A group of people who individually can do nothing, but as a group decide that nothing can be done.
— Fred Allen

Bureaucracy is a giant mechanism operated by pygmies.

— HONORÉ DE BALZAC

Structure cannot be avoided. If you don't create your own structure, you have to deal with someone else's.

— LAURENCE G. BOLDT

When administration and orders are inconsistent, the men's spirits are low, and the officers exceedingly angry.

— CHANG YU

Large organization is loose organization. Nay, it would be almost as true to say that organization is always disorganization.

— G. K. CHESTERTON

A committee is a cul-de-sac down which ideas are lured and then quietly strangled.   — BARNETT COCKS

Focusing on a product is time telling—a leader may be very good at it, but once that leader is gone, the company may be left with no one else who can do it. Creating a company is clock building—a leader creates a system that can always tell the time, no matter who's in charge.

— JIM COLLINS AND JERRY PORRAS

An empowered organization is one in which individuals have the knowledge, skill, desire, and opportunity to personally succeed in a way that leads to collective organizational success.   — STEPHEN R. COVEY

Trust in organizations depends on the reasonable assumption by followers that leaders can be depended on to do the right thing.   — MAX DEPREE

The only things that evolve by themselves in an organization are disorder, friction and malperformance.

— PETER DRUCKER

No grand idea was ever born in a conference, but a lot of foolish ideas have died there.

— F. SCOTT FITZGERALD

Synergy means behavior of whole systems unpredicted by the behavior of their parts.

— R. BUCKMINSTER FULLER

The single most important factor in determining the climate of an organization is the top executive.

— CHARLES GALLOWAY

The safest way I know for changing the character of any institution is through building a staff of very able people who will get their greatest creative fulfillment in finding and installing good solutions to critical problems.

— ROBERT GREENLEAF

A committee is an animal with four back legs.

— JOHN LE CARRÉ

If we do not concern ourselves with how we can rule organizations, the organizations will rule us.

— J. KEITH LOUDEN

The only thing that saves us from the bureaucracy is inefficiency. An efficient bureaucracy is the greatest threat to liberty.

— EUGENE MCCARTHY

The longer the title, the less important the job.

— GEORGE MCGOVERN

Paperwork is the embalming fluid of bureaucracy, maintaining an appearance of life where none exists.

— ROBERT J. MELTZER

The ideal committee is one with me as chairman, and two other members in bed with flu. — LORD MILVERTON

Organizations don't have tops and bottoms. These are just misguided metaphors. What organizations really have are the *outer* people, connected to the world, and the *inner* ones, disconnected from it, as well as many so called *middle* managers, who are desperately trying to connect the inner and outer people to each other. — HENRY MINTZBERG

Nothing is possible without men; nothing is lasting without institutions.
— JEAN MONNET, FATHER OF THE EUROPEAN ECONOMIC COMMUNITY

In the infancy of societies, the chiefs of the state shape its institutions; later the institutions shape the chiefs of state.
— MONTESQUIEU

If there is a single vital skill the successful manager must have, it is the skill to manage a meeting effectively.
— ROGER MOSVICK AND ROBERT NELSON

I do not rule Russia; ten thousand clerks do.
— NICHOLAS I

In a hierarchy every employee tends to rise to his level of incompetence. . . . In time every post tends to be occupied by an employee who is incompetent to carry out its duties. . . . Work is accomplished by those employees who have not yet reached their level of incompetence.
— LAURENCE PETER

Bureaucrats write memoranda both because they appear to be busy when they are writing and because their memos, once written, immediately become proof that they were busy.

— CHARLES PETERS

We trained hard . . . but every time we were beginning to form up into teams, we would be reorganized. I was to learn later in life that we tend to meet any new situation by reorganizing . . . and a wonderful method it can be for creating the illusion of progress while producing inefficiency and demoralization.

— PETRONIUS, FIRST CENTURY

Bureaucracy does not take kindly to being assailed and isn't above using a few low blows and a knee to the groin when it fights back. Knowing this, I have become extremely cautious in dealing with government agencies.

— RONALD REAGAN

If you're going to sin, sin against God, not the bureaucracy. God will forgive you but the bureaucracy won't.

— HYMAN RICKOVER

The way a team plays as a whole determines its success. You may have the greatest bunch of individual stars in the world, but if they don't play together, the club won't be worth a dime.

— BABE RUTH

Even weak men when united are powerful.

—JOHANN FRIEDRICH VON SCHILLER

Responsibility equals accountability equals ownership. And a sense of ownership is one of the most important weapons a team or organization can have.

— PAT SUMMIT

If you ever live in a country run by a committee, be on the committee. — WILLIAM GRAHAM SUMNER

When the common soldiers are too strong and their officers too weak, the result is *insubordination*. When the officers are too strong and the common soldiers too weak, the result is *collapse*. — SUN TZU

Any fool can make a rule.

— HENRY DAVID THOREAU

When conditions of any organization are changed, the whole organization will shift in an attempt to restore the original condition. — UNKNOWN

PATIENCE

If you are patient in one moment of anger, you will escape a hundred days of sorrow. — CHINESE PROVERB

Patience is power; with time and patience the mulberry leaf becomes silk. — CHINESE PROVERB

To know how to wait is the great secret of success.

— JOSEPH DE MAISTRE

Talent is long patience.

— GUSTAVE FLAUBERT

Great things are not done by impulse but by a series of small things brought together. — VINCENT VAN GOGH

Patience has its limits. Take it too far and it's cowardice.

— GEORGE JACKSON

Everything must wait its turn . . . peach blossoms for the second month and chrysanthemums for the ninth.

— JAPANESE PROVERB

Experience has taught me this, that we undo ourselves by impatience.

— MICHEL DE MONTAIGNE

Patience and diligence, like faith, remove mountains.

— WILLIAM PENN

Wisely and slow. They stumble that run fast.

— WILLIAM SHAKESPEARE, *ROMEO AND JULIET*

Patience serves as a protection against wrongs as clothes do against cold. For if you put on more clothes as the cold increases, it will have no power to hurt you. So in like manner you must grow in patience when you meet with great wrongs, and they will then be powerless to vex your mind.

— LEONARDO DA VINCI

See also Persistence

PEOPLE SKILLS

No one doth well what he doth against his will.

— SAINT AUGUSTINE

I don't want people who want to dance. I want people who have to dance.

— GEORGE BALANCHINE

Show me a man who cannot bother to do little things and I'll show you a man who cannot be trusted to do big things.

— Lawrence D. Bell

None of us is as smart as all of us.

— Kenneth Blanchard (also attributed to others)

A chief does not rule land, he rules people.

— Buganda proverb (East Africa)

Behind an able man there are always other able men.

— Chinese proverb

People whose talents are not exploited become disenchanted and disruptive.

— Terence Conran

Morale is the greatest single factor in successful war.

— Dwight D. Eisenhower

The last thing I would ever ask any man that I appoint to a high office is what are going to be his decisions in specific cases.

— Dwight D. Eisenhower

In order to *willingly* accept the direction of another individual, it *must* feel good to do so. This business of making another person feel good in the unspectacular course of his daily comings and goings is, in my view, the very essence of leadership.

— Irwin Federman

There is no such thing as an insignificant human being. To treat people that way is a kind of sin and there's no reason for it. None.

— Debbi Fields

People are not motivated by failure; they are motivated by achievement and recognition.   — F. F. FOURNIES

If you want something really important to be done you must not merely satisfy the reason, you must move the heart also.
                                            — MAHATMA GANDHI

Treat people as if they were what they ought to be and you help them to become what they are capable of being.
                                      — JOHANN WOLFGANG VON GOETHE

Few great men could pass Personnel.
                                            — PAUL GOODMAN

Avoid victories over superiors.
                                         — BALTASAR GRACIÁN

All appointments hurt. Five friends are made cold or hostile for every appointment; no new friends are made. All patronage is perilous to men of real ability or merit. It aids only those who lack other claims to public support.
                                         — RUTHERFORD B. HAYES

I try to set standards that'll make other people wish they were on my team.   — KEN HORNE

In the end, all business operations can be reduced to three words: people, product and profits. People come first. Unless you've got a good team, you can't do much with the other two.   — LEE IACCOCA

The deepest principle in human nature is the craving to be appreciated.   — WILLIAM JAMES

Be kind, for everyone you meet is fighting a hard battle.

— PHILO JUDAEUS

People may . . . do satisfactory work . . . because they are forced to. They only do *superior* work because they *want* to.

— DENNIS KINLAW

You're only as good as the people you hire.

— RAY KROC

Never give a man up until he has failed at something he likes.

— LEWIS E. LAWES

You get more of the behavior you reward. You don't get what you hope for, ask for, wish for, or beg for. You get what you reward.

— MICHEL LE BOEUF

There are no ordinary people. You have never talked to an ordinary mortal. . . . It is immortals whom we joke with, work with, marry, snub and exploit—immortal horrors or everlasting splendors. . . . Next to the Blessed Sacrament itself, your neighbor is the holiest object presented to your senses.

— C. S. LEWIS

I hold it more important to have the players' confidence than their affection.

— VINCE LOMBARDI

Natural talent, intelligence, a wonderful education—none of these guarantees success. Something else is needed: the sensitivity to understand what other people want and the willingness to give it to them.

— JOHN LUTHER

Leaders must be close enough to relate to others, but far enough ahead to motivate them.

— JOHN C. MAXWELL

The only way to keep the goodwill and high esteem of the people you work with is to deserve it. No one can fool all of the people all of the time. Each of us, eventually, is recognized for exactly what we are—not what we try to appear to be.

— John C. Maxwell

Finish each transaction as if you expect to do business with them tomorrow.

— August Meyer

We should ever conduct ourselves towards our enemy as if he were one day to be our friend.

— Cardinal Newman

What upsets me is not that you lied to me, but that from now on I can no longer believe you.

— Friedrich Nietzsche

The art of dealing with people is the foremost secret of successful men. A man's success in handling people is the very yardstick by which the outcome of his whole life's work is measured.

— Paul C. Packer

Never tell people how to do things. Tell them what to do and they will surprise you with their ingenuity.

— George S. Patton

You can impress people from a distance. You can impact people only from up close.

— Will Richert

I will pay more for the ability to deal with people than any other ability under the sun.

— John D. Rockefeller

The best leader is the one who has sense enough to pick good men to do what he wants done, and self-restraint enough to keep from meddling with them while they do it.

— Theodore Roosevelt

First-rate people hire first-rate people; second-rate people hire third-rate people.
— LEO ROSTEN

I consider my ability to arouse enthusiasm among men the greatest asset I possess, and the way to develop the best that is in a man is by appreciation and encouragement, so I am anxious to praise but loath to find fault. If I like anything, I am hearty in my appreciation and lavish in my praise.
— CHARLES SCHWAB

I've yet to find the man, however exalted his station, who did not do better work and put forth greater effort under a spirit of approval than under the spirit of criticism.
— CHARLES SCHWAB

Ill can he rule the great that cannot reach the small.
— EDMUND SPENSER

Country judge, chairman of a committee, President of the U.S.: they are all the same kind of jobs. It is the business of dealing with people.
— HARRY S. TRUMAN

People don't do what we expect; they do what we inspect.
— UNKNOWN

Appreciation is a wonderful thing: it makes what is excellent in others belong to us as well.
— VOLTAIRE

My most important contribution to IBM was my ability to pick strong and intelligent men and then hold the team together by persuasion, by apologies, by financial incentives, by speeches, by chatting with their wives, by thoughtfulness when they were sick . . . and by using every tool at my command to make that team think I was a decent guy.
— THOMAS J. WATSON

Every man who takes office in Washington either grows or swells, and when I give a man office I watch him carefully to see whether he is growing or swelling. — WOODROW WILSON

I use not only all the brains I have, but all I can borrow.

— WOODROW WILSON

See also Mentoring; Talent

PERSISTENCE

All rising to great places is by a winding stair.

— FRANCIS BACON

For though a righteous man falls seven times, he rises again.

— THE BIBLE, PROVERBS 24:16

Victory belongs to the most persevering.

— NAPOLEON BONAPARTE

Never give in, never give in, never, never, never.

— WINSTON CHURCHILL

Press on. Nothing can take the place of persistence. Talent will not. Nothing is more common than unsuccessful men with talent. Genius will not. Unrewarded genius is almost a proverb. Education will not. The world is full of educated derelicts. Persistence and determination alone are overwhelmingly powerful. — CALVIN COOLIDGE

Never say die.

— CHARLES DICKENS

There must be a beginning of any great matter, but the continuing unto the end until it be thoroughly finished yields the true glory. — SIR FRANCIS DRAKE

Persistent people begin their success where others end in failure. — EDWARD EGGLESTON

I think and think, for months, for years; ninety-nine times the conclusion is false. The hundredth time I am right. — ALBERT EINSTEIN

In the realm of ideas everything depends on enthusiasm; in the real world, all rests on perseverance. — JOHANN WOLFGANG VON GOETHE

Great works are performed not by strength but by perseverance. — SAMUEL JOHNSON

Keep on going and the chances are that you will stumble on something, perhaps when you are least expecting it. I have never heard of anyone stumbling on something sitting down. — CHARLES F. KETTERING

It's easy to have faith in yourself and have discipline when you're a winner, when you're number one. What you got to have is faith and discipline when you're not a winner. — VINCE LOMBARDI

The virtue lies in the struggle, not in the prize. — RICHARD MILNES

PERSISTENCE

I am not an optimist. I am simply persistent. . . . I can wait a long time for the right moment. In Cognac they are good at waiting. It is the only way to make good brandy.

— JEAN MONNET, EUROPEAN ECONOMIC COMMUNITY LEADER, WHOSE FAMILY MAKES BRANDY IN COGNAC, FRANCE

Let me tell you the secret that has led me to my goal. My strength lies solely in my tenacity. — LOUIS PASTEUR

If at first you don't succeed, you are running about average.
— UNKNOWN

To win the race is to rise each time we fall.
— UNKNOWN

Obstacles cannot crush me. Every obstacle yields to stern resolve. He who is fixed to a star does not change his mind.
— LEONARDO DA VINCI

Persevere and preserve yourself for better circumstances.
— VIRGIL

Perseverance is everything.
— YORUBA PROVERB

See also Difficulties; Patience; Success

PERSPECTIVE

You are not in charge of the universe; you are in charge of yourself. — A. BENNETT

Count no day lost in which you waited your turn, took only your share and sought advantage over no one.

— ROBERT BRAULT

It's strange, but wherever I take my eyes, they always see things from my point of view.

— ASHLEIGH BRILLIANT

One sees great things from the valley, only small things from the peak.

— G. K. CHESTERTON

It is well to remember that the entire population of the universe, with one trifling exception, is composed of others.

— JOHN ANDREW HOLMES

Is it worth the lion's while to terrify the mouse?

— CARL JUNG

Winning is overemphasized. The only time it is really important is in surgery and war.

— AL McGUIRE

Just because your voice reaches halfway around the world doesn't mean you are wiser than when it reached only to the end of the bar.

— EDWARD R. MURROW

The problem . . . is not that we cannot do it all, but that we *want* to do it all. I am increasingly convinced that many of our guilt feelings are based on our Messianic aspirations, our desire to be God and take over his work.

— HENRI NOUWEN

Don't forget that the fifty or so invitations you receive a week are sent not because those people are just dying to see you, but because of the position you hold. If you don't believe me, ask one of your predecessors how fast they stop.

— DONALD RUMSFELD

When you get to be President, there are all those things, the honors, the twenty-one gun salutes, all those things. You have to remember it isn't for you. It's for the presidency.

— HARRY S. TRUMAN

There is only one boss—the customer. And he can fire everybody in the company from the chairman on down, simply by spending his money somewhere else. — SAM WALTON

PLANNING

The finest plans are always ruined by the littleness of those who ought to carry them out, for the Emperor himself can actually do nothing. — BERTOLT BRECHT

One possible reason why things aren't going according to plan is that there never was a plan. — ASHLEIGH BRILLIANT

Make no little plans; they have no magic to stir men's blood.

— DANIEL H. BURNHAM

We plan long range to know what to achieve today, this week, this month. The reason we look three years ahead is to know what to accomplish now. — KENNON CALLAHAN

If you are planning for one year, grow rice. If you are planning for 20 years, grow trees. If you are planning for centuries, grow men. — CHINESE PROVERB

Strategic planning is necessary precisely because we cannot forecast. . . . Strategic planning does not deal with future decisions. It deals with the futurity of present decisions. Decisions exist only in the present. The question that faces the strategic decision-maker is not what his organization should do tomorrow. It is: "What do we have to do today to be ready for an uncertain tomorrow?" — PETER DRUCKER

Plans are nothing. Planning is everything.

— DWIGHT D. EISENHOWER

A bad beginning makes a bad ending.

— EURIPIDES

It is best to do things systematically, since we are only human and disorder is our worst enemy. — HESIOD

Good results without good planning come from good luck, not good management. — DAVID JAQUITH

Every minute spent in planning will save two in execution.

— HENRY KAISER

Lay plans for the accomplishment of the difficult before it becomes difficult; make something big by starting with it when it is small. Be as careful at the end as the beginning and there will be no ruined enterprises. — LAO-TZU

If we can know where we are and something about how we got there, we might see where we are trending, and if the outcomes which lie naturally in our course are unacceptable, make timely change. — ABRAHAM LINCOLN

It wasn't raining when Noah built the ark.

— HOWARD RUFF

Our plans miscarry because they have no aim. When a man does not know what harbor he is making for, no wind is the right wind.

— SENECA

Gresham's Law of Planning [is] that routine drives out non-programmed activity.

— H. A. SIMON

It's a bad plan that can't be changed.

— PUBLILIUS SYRUS

No plan survives contact with the enemy.

— UNKNOWN

Before you build a better mousetrap, it helps to know if there are any mice out there.

— MORTIMER ZUCKERMAN

POWER AND AUTHORITY

Power tends to corrupt, and absolute power corrupts absolutely.

— LORD ACTON

I am more and more convinced that man is a dangerous creature; and that power, whether vested in many or a few, is ever grasping, and like the grave, cries "Give, give!"

— ABIGAIL ADAMS

It is weakness rather than wickedness which renders men unfit to be trusted with unlimited power.

— JOHN ADAMS

Knowledge is power.

— FRANCIS BACON

The decision as to whether an order has authority or not lies with the person to whom it is addressed, and does not reside in "persons of authority" or those who issue orders.

— CHESTER I. BARNARD

Greatness lies not so much in being strong but in the right use of strength.   — HENRY WARD BEECHER

We thought, because we had power, we had wisdom.

— STEPHEN VINCENT BENÉT

Power gradually extirpates from the mind every humane and gentle virtue.   — EDMUND BURKE

Power intoxicates men. It is never voluntarily surrendered. It must be taken from them.   — JAMES F. BYRNES

Power, like lightning, injures before its warning.

— CALDERÓN

Power without a nation's confidence is nothing.

— CATHERINE THE GREAT

It is a fine thing to command, even if it be only a herd of cattle.   — MIGUEL DE CERVANTES

Power will intoxicate the best hearts, as wine the strongest heads. No man is wise enough, nor good enough, to be trusted with unlimited power.   — CHARLES CALEB COLTON

To know the pains of power, we must go to those who have it; to know its pleasures, we must go to those who are seeking it: the pains of power are real, its pleasures imaginary.

— CHARLES CALEB COLTON

Power is the ability to make changes.

— HUGH CULLMAN

There can be no power without mystery. There must always be a "something" which others cannot altogether fathom, which puzzles them, stirs them, and rivets their attention.

— CHARLES DE GAULLE

All executive power—from the reign of ancient kings to the rule of modern dictators—has the outward appearance of efficiency.

— WILLIAM O. DOUGLAS

Don't let your will roar when your power only whispers.

— THOMAS FULLER

Power is of two kinds: one is obtained by the fear of punishment and the other by acts of love.

— MAHATMA GANDHI

The sole advantage of power is that you can do more good.

— BALTASAR GRACIÁN

Power may justly be compared to a great river; while kept within its bounds it is both beautiful and useful, but when it overflows its banks, it is then too impetuous to be stemmed; it bears down all before it, and brings destruction and desolation wherever it comes.

— ANDREW HAMILTON

Only he deserves power who every day justifies it.

— DAG HAMMARSKJÖLD

Unused power slips imperceptibly into the hands of another.
— Konrad Heiden

The more power you give away, the more you have.
— Frances Hesselbein

The only prize much cared for by the powerful is power. The prize of the general is not a bigger tent, but command.
— Oliver Wendell Holmes Jr.

[Power] is . . . the ability not to have to please.
— Elizabeth Janeway

It is easier to talk about money—and much easier to talk about sex—than it is to talk about power. People who have it deny it; people who want it do not want to appear to hunger for it; and people who engage in its machinations do so secretly.
— Rosabeth Moss Kanter

Power is like the old Esso ad—a tiger in your tank. But you can't let the tiger out, you just let people hear him roar. You use power terribly sparingly because it has a short half-life. You let people know you have it and hope that you don't have to use it.
— William P. Kelly

The management of a balance of power is a permanent undertaking.
— Henry Kissinger

Power is the ultimate aphrodisiac.
— Henry Kissinger

Power lasts 10 years, influence not more than a hundred.
— Korean proverb

The great question which, in all ages, has disturbed mankind and brought on them the greatest part of those mischiefs which have ruined cities, depopulated countries, and disordered the peace of the world, has been, not whether there be power in the world, not whence it came, but who should have it.

— JOHN LOCKE

Today the real test of power is not capacity to make war but capacity to prevent it.

— ANNE O'HARE MCCORMICK

It is always a great mistake to command when you are not sure you will be obeyed.

— COMTE DE MIRABEAU

He is the best of men who dislikes power.

— MOHAMMED

Power is not a means, it is an end. One does not establish a dictatorship in order to safeguard a revolution; one makes the revolution in order to establish the dictatorship.

— GEORGE ORWELL

No extraordinary power should be lodged in any one individual.

— THOMAS PAINE

Justice and power must be brought together, so that whatever is just may be powerful, and whatever is powerful may be just.

— BLAISE PASCAL

The measure of a man is what he does with power.

— PITTACUS

Power always has to be kept in check; power exercised in secret, especially under the cloak of national security, is doubly dangerous.

— WILLIAM PROXMIRE

Power breeds isolation. Isolation leads to the capricious use of power. In turn, the capricious use of power breaks down the normal channels of communication between the leader and the people whom he leads. This ultimately means the deterioration of power and with it the capacity to sustain unity in our society. This is the problem we face today.

— GEORGE REEDY

Fortunately, there are still those among us who have a healthy irreverence toward power, even as they seek it. — WEIR REID

Power undirected by high purpose spells calamity; and high purpose by itself is utterly useless if the power to put it into effect is lacking. — THEODORE ROOSEVELT

The least one can say of power is that a vocation for it is suspicious. — JEAN ROSTAND

The power to define the situation is the ultimate power.

— JERRY RUBIN

He who has great power should use it lightly.

— SENECA

Power, like a desolating pestilence,
Pollutes whate'er it touches.

— PERCY BYSSHE SHELLEY

Power corrupts, but lack of power corrupts absolutely.

— ADLAI STEVENSON

Power acquired by guilt has seldom been directed to any good end or useful purpose. — TACITUS

Being powerful is like being a lady. If you have to tell people
you are, you aren't. — MARGARET THATCHER

We have, I fear, confused power with greatness.
— STEWART L. UDALL

Power means not needing to raise your voice.
— GEORGE F. WILL

Power is the capacity of some persons to produce intended
and foreseen effects on others. — DENNIS WRONG

PREPARATION

Preparation can be defined in three words: Leave Nothing
Undone. — GEORGE ALLEN

When you want position, beware of position. But when you
are called because you are worthy, when you are startled at the
call, you can afford to take the place in life that beckons and
bids you come.
— MARTIN GROVE BRUMBAUGH, PRESIDENT OF JUNIATA COLLEGE;
COMMENCEMENT ADDRESS, 1898

The man who is prepared has his battle half-fought.
— MIGUEL DE CERVANTES

You can't hope to be lucky. You have to prepare to be lucky.
— TIMOTHY DOWD

In the crises of our life . . . our words show where our souls
have been feeding. — HARRY EMERSON FOSDICK

No matter who you are, no matter how good an athlete you are, we're creatures of habit. The better your habits are, the better they'll be in pressure situations. — WAYNE GRETZKY

The only real training for leadership is leadership.

— ANTHONY JAY

When the press talks about my successes as Senate majority leader they always emphasize my capacity to persuade, to wheel and deal. Hardly anyone ever mentions that I usually had more and better information than my colleagues.

— LYNDON B. JOHNSON

The key is not the "will to win". . . . Everybody has that. It is the will to *prepare* to win that is important. — BOBBY KNIGHT

I will study and get ready and then maybe the chance will come. — ABRAHAM LINCOLN

Chance favors the prepared mind.

— LOUIS PASTEUR

The single most important foundation for any leader is a solid academic background in history. That discipline gives perspective to the problems of the present and drives home the point that there is really very little new under the sun.

— JAMES BOND STOCKDALE

People always told me that my natural ability and good eyesight were the reasons for my success as a hitter. They never talk about the practice, practice, practice. — TED WILLIAMS

See also Opportunities

PRESSURES AND TEMPTATIONS

The temptation comes in different forms for different leaders, but the top three have always been money, sex and power. Do whatever you need to do to avoid stupidity in these and other areas of weakness.
— LEITH ANDERSON

Truth has a way of shifting under pressure.
— CURTIS BOK

I believe that the number one leadership sin is that of top-down autocratic arrogance.
— HANS FINZEL

Not all that tempts your wand'ring eyes
And heedless hearts, is lawful prize;
Nor all that glisters, gold.
— THOMAS GRAY

I worry until midnight and from then on I let God worry.
— LOUIS GUANELLA

Never bear more than one trouble at a time. Some people bear three kinds: all they have had, all they have now, and all they expect to have.
— EVERETT HALE

What makes resisting temptation difficult, for many people, is that they don't want to discourage it completely.
— FRANKLIN P. JONES

He who is firmly seated in authority soon learns to think security, and not progress, the highest lesson of statecraft.
— JAMES RUSSELL LOWELL

Everyone wants my blood but no one wants my job.

— GUY MOLLETT

'Tis one thing to be tempted, Escalus, another thing to fall.

— WILLIAM SHAKESPEARE, *MEASURE FOR MEASURE*

The bow too tensely strung is easily broken.

— PUBLILIUS SYRUS

A man is led the way he wishes to follow.

— THE TALMUD

Temptation rarely comes in working hours. It is in their leisure time that men are made or marred.   — W. M. TAYLOR

If you have been tempted into evil, fly from it. It is not falling into the water, but lying in it, that drowns.   — UNKNOWN

Ever notice that the whisper of temptation can be heard farther than the loudest call to duty?   — EARL WILSON

He who loves praise loves temptation.

— THOMAS WILSON

See also Crises; Critics and Criticism; Difficulties; Hope and Despair

PRIORITIES

Stop spending dollar time on penny jobs.

— MARY KAY ASH (OF MARY KAY COSMETICS)

What good is it for a man to gain the whole world, yet forfeit his soul? — THE BIBLE, MARK 8:36

You cannot protect your priorities unless you learn to decline, tactfully but firmly, every request that does not contribute to the achievement of your goals. — ED BLISS

Our grand business is, not to see what lies dimly at a distance, but to do what lies closely at hand. — THOMAS CARLYLE

In the discharge of the duties of the office, there is one rule of action more important than all the others. It consists of never doing anything that someone else can do for you. — CALVIN COOLIDGE

Next to knowing when to seize an opportunity, the most important thing in life is to know when to forego an advantage. — BENJAMIN DISRAELI

Concentrate first on doing the right things, then on doing things right. There is nothing so wasteful as doing the wrong things well. — PETER DRUCKER

O Lord, may I be directed what to do and what to leave undone. — ELIZABETH FRY

He that is everywhere is nowhere. — THOMAS FULLER

What is the use of running when you are on the wrong road? — GERMAN PROVERB

The dog has four feet, but he does not walk them in four roads. — HAITIAN PROVERB

Two essential qualities in a good organizer are a thorough and constant perception of the end in view, and a power of dealing with masses of details, never forgetting that they are details, and not becoming their slave. — ARTHUR HELPS

One half of knowing what you want is knowing what you must give up before you get it. — SIDNEY HOWARD

I'm constantly amazed by the number of people who can't seem to control their own schedules. Over the years, I've had many executives come to me and say with pride, "Boy, last year I worked so hard that I didn't take any vacation." It's actually nothing to be proud of. I always feel like responding, "You dummy. You mean to tell me that you can take responsibility for an $80 million project, and you can't plan two weeks out of the year to go off with your family and have some fun?" — LEE IACOCCA

Keep in mind that you are always saying "no" to something. If it isn't to the apparent, urgent things in your life, it is probably to the most fundamental, highly important things. Even when the urgent is good, the good can keep you from your best, keep you from your unique contribution, if you let it.

— HELEN KELLER

Besides the noble art of getting things done, there is the noble art of leaving things undone. The wisdom of life consists in the elimination of nonessentials. — LIN YUTANG

I claim not to have controlled events, but confess plainly that events have controlled me. — ABRAHAM LINCOLN

[A leader is one who] must always conserve his resources for the battles that count. He must look at the major objectives of his administration . . . and must never become involved in a fight on a minor issue which might prejudice his chance to win on a major issue. — RICHARD M. NIXON

What may be done at any time will be done at no time.
— SCOTTISH PROVERB

In your area of responsibility, if you do not control events, you are at the mercy of events. — HARLAND SVARE

Don't spend ten dollars' worth of energy on a ten-cent problem. . . . There are millions of want-to's and have-to's in life. Ultimately, these pressures create stress only when your time and energy-spending decisions aren't consistent with your goals, beliefs and values. — DONALD A. TUBESING

You can't steal second base and keep one foot on first.
— UNIDENTIFIED EXECUTIVE

See also Goals; Opportunities; Self-Renewal

PROBLEMS AND PROBLEM SOLVING

To be always ready, a man must be able to cut a knot, for not everything can be untied. — HENRI FREDERIC AMIEL

Ninety-nine percent of problems are like sparks; they will burn out if they are not fanned. The early approach of leaders should be to keep conflicts calm. — LEITH ANDERSON

Most problems have either many answers or no answer. Only a few problems have a single answer. — EDMUND C. BERKELEY

If there are obstacles, the shortest line between two points may be the crooked line. — BERTOLT BRECHT

It isn't that they can't see the solution. It is that they can't see the problem. — G. K. CHESTERTON

Do not dress in leaf-made clothes when going to put out a fire. — CHINESE PROVERB

When solving problems, dig at the roots instead of just hacking at the leaves. — ANTHONY J. D'ANGELO

Outline a problem as clearly as possible and you've already half-solved it. — JOHN DEWEY

The measure of success is not whether you have a tough problem to deal with, but whether it's the same problem you had last year. — JOHN FOSTER DULLES

Unlike presidential administrations, problems rarely have terminal dates. — DWIGHT D. EISENHOWER

All cases are unique and very similar to others. — T. S. ELIOT

Nothing is particularly hard if you divide it into small jobs. — HENRY FORD

Lift your consciousness above the level where you met the problem. — EMMET FOX

The only way round is through.

— ROBERT FROST

If you are in a shipwreck and all the boats are gone, a piano top buoyant enough to keep you afloat may come along and make a fortuitous life preserver. This is not to say, though, that the best way to design a life preserver is in the form of a piano top. I think that we are clinging to a great many piano tops in accepting yesterday's fortuitous contrivings as constituting the only means for solving a given problem.

— R. BUCKMINSTER FULLER

When I am working on a problem, I never think about beauty. I only think about how to solve the problem . . . but, when I have finished, if the solution is not beautiful, I know it is wrong.

— R. BUCKMINSTER FULLER

Problems are messages.

— SHAKTI GAWAIN

It is not always by plugging away at a difficulty and sticking to it that one overcomes it; often it is by working on the one next to it. Some things and some people have to be approached obliquely, at an angle.

— ANDRÉ GIDE

We will either find a way, or make one.

— HANNIBAL

When tempted to "fight fire with fire," remember that the fire department usually uses water.

— S. I. HAYAKAWA

In a complex social system, a problem will lack clarity because a multitude of factions will have divergent opinions about both the nature of the problem and its possible solutions.

— RONALD A. HEIFETZ

Problems worthy of attack prove their worth by hitting back.
— PIET HEIN

The second assault on the same problem should come from a totally different direction. — TOM HIRSHFIELD

A good problem statement often includes: (a) what is known, (b) what is unknown, and (c) what is sought.
— EDWARD HODNETT

The more choices you have, the better your solution to a problem is likely to be. As you start your attack on a problem, therefore, you keep asking, not merely, "Is there another alternative?" You ask, "How many more alternatives are there?" The difference between the fair problem solver and the first-rate one shows up here. — EDWARD HODNETT

One kind of problem that taxes our ability to ask the right questions is the problem that drifts in like fog, very gradually, until visibility has dropped to near zero. Some gradual change in conditions has occurred, and by the time the situation has become serious enough to gain everyone's attention its critical elements may be lost to view.
— CHARLES KEPNER AND BENJAMIN TREGOE

Problems are the price of progress. Don't bring me anything but trouble. Good news weakens me. — CHARLES F. KETTERING

Each success only buys an admission ticket to a more difficult problem. — HENRY KISSINGER

The biggest problem in the world could have been solved when it was small. — LAO-TZU

Insanity is doing the same thing in the same way and expecting different results.
— LAO-TZU

Quiet calm deliberation disentangles every knot.
— HAROLD MACMILLAN

I must have assistants who will solve their own problems and tell me later what they have done.
— GEORGE C. MARSHALL

When the only tool you have is a hammer, you tend to treat everything as if it were a nail.
— ABRAHAM MASLOW

Some problems are so difficult they can't be solved in a million years—unless someone thinks about them for five minutes.
— H. L. MENCKEN

Many a problem will solve itself if you'll forget it and go fishing.
— OLIN MILLER

It is in the whole process of meeting and solving problems that life has meaning. Problems are the cutting edge that distinguishes between success and failure. Problems call forth our courage and our wisdom; indeed, they create our courage and our wisdom. It is only because of problems that we grow mentally and spiritually. It is through the pain of confronting and resolving problems that we learn.
— M. SCOTT PECK

The solution to a problem changes the problem.
— JOHN PEERS

All difficult problems have easy, simple, understandable, wrong solutions.
— LAURENCE PETER

In all the creative work that I have done, what has come first is a problem, a puzzle involving discomfort. Then comes concentrated voluntary application entailing great effort. After this, a period without conscious thought, and finally a solution bringing with it the complete plan of a book. This last stage is usually sudden and seems to be the important moment for subsequent achievement. — BERTRAND RUSSELL

I sometimes indulge in Solitaire. For a mindless game, it provides many useful lessons: if the deal is bad — walk away at the outset. If you are greedy, you'll be sorry later. Most importantly: some situations just do not have a solution.
— CHARLES SIMONYI, CHIEF ARCHITECT, MICROSOFT

A problem is something you have hopes of changing. Anything else is a fact of life. — C. R. SMITH

Find the essence of each situation, like a logger clearing a log jam. The pro climbs a tall tree and locates the key log, blows it, and lets the stream do the rest. An amateur would start at the edge of the jam and move all the logs, eventually moving the key log. Both approaches work, but the "essence" concept saves time and effort. Almost all problems have a "key" log if we learn to find it. — FRED SMITH

By being the problem solver of last resort, the leader can help the organization grow and thrive. — PERRY SMITH

It is a common experience that a problem difficult at night is resolved in the morning after the committee of sleep has worked on it. — JOHN STEINBECK

Our greatest problems in life come not so much from the situations we confront, as from our doubts about our ability to handle them.
— SUSAN TAYLOR

Intractable problems are usually not intractable because there are no solutions, but because there are no solutions without severe side effects. . . . It is only when we demand a solution with no costs that there are no solutions.
— LESTER C. THUROW

I have learned to use the word impossible with the greatest caution.
— WERNHER VON BRAUN

You can't solve a problem? Well, get down and investigate the present facts and the problem's past history. When you have investigated the problem thoroughly, you will know how to solve it.
— MAO ZEDONG

See also Clear Thinking; Creativity; Crises; Difficulties

RESPONSIBILITY

The price of power is responsibility for the public good.
— WINTHROP W. ALDRICH

From everyone who has been given much, much will be demanded; and from the one who has been entrusted with much, much more will be asked.
— THE BIBLE, LUKE 12:48

It is not by whining that one carries out the job of king.
— NAPOLEON BONAPARTE

When the Emperor errs, the peasant shivers.

— CHINESE PROVERB

The price of greatness is responsibility.

— WINSTON CHURCHILL

A good leader takes a little more than his share of blame, a little less than his share of credit.

— ARNOLD H. GLASGOW

To let oneself be bound by a duty from the moment you see it approaching is part of the integrity that alone justifies responsibility.

— DAG HAMMARSKJÖLD

There are plenty of recommendations on how to get out of trouble cheaply and fast. Most of them come down to this: Deny your responsibility.

— LYNDON B. JOHNSON

I know that when things don't go well, they like to blame the president, and that is one of the things presidents are paid for.

— JOHN F. KENNEDY

God obliges no man to more than he has given him ability to perform.

— THE KORAN

Responsibility gravitates to the power that can carry out that responsibility. If you alone can do what ought to be done, then that oughtness rests on you. You can't dodge it. It is yours.

— LYNN LANDRUM

No snowflake in an avalanche ever feels responsible.

— STANISLAW LEC

I am compelled to take a more impartial and unprejudiced view of things. Without claiming to be your superior, which I do not, my position enables me to understand my duty in all these matters better than you possibly can, and I hope you do not yet doubt my integrity.

— Abraham Lincoln

I attribute my success to this: I never gave or took an excuse.

— Florence Nightingale

Don't feel totally, personally, irrevocably responsible for everything; that's my job. — God

— Sign on a pastor's desk

The ability to accept responsibility is the measure of the man.

— Roy L. Smith

When you have once taken up a responsibility, you must see it through.

— Rabindranath Tagore

Our life is a gift from God. What we do with our life is our gift to God.

— Unknown

Few things help an individual more than to place responsibility upon him, and to let him know that you trust him.

— Booker T. Washington

The most important thought I ever had was that of my individual responsibility to God.

— Daniel Webster

RESULTS

Leave results to God.

— Elizabeth Barrett Browning

It's no use saying "we are doing our best." You have got to succeed in doing what is necessary. — WINSTON CHURCHILL

Results! Why, man, I have gotten a lot of results. I know several thousand things that won't work. — THOMAS EDISON

You can't build a reputation on what you're going to do.
— HENRY FORD

What gets measured gets done.
— MASON HAIRE

It is not enough to aim; you must hit.
— ITALIAN PROVERB

Better to do a little well than a great deal badly.
— SOCRATES

Too many people substitute effort for accomplishment. The reason for working is to get *results*. The person who gets the most results is working smarter and harder. Fatigue is not an indicator of success. — ZIG ZIGLAR

See also Success

RISK

There is only one danger I find in life—you may take too many precautions. — ALFRED ADLER

No one tests the depth of a river with both his feet.
— ASHANTI PROVERB

A ship in port is safe, but that is not what ships are built for.

— BENAZIR BHUTTO

There is no way to catch a snake that is as safe as not catching him.

— JACOB M. BRAUDE

One thing I know . . . is this: spend it all, shoot it, play it, lose it, all, right away, every time. Do not hoard what seems good for [later]; give it, give it all, give it now. . . . Anything you do not give freely and abundantly becomes lost to you. You open your safe and find ashes.

— ANNIE DILLARD

People who don't take risks generally make about two big mistakes a year. People who do take risks generally make about two big mistakes a year.

— PETER DRUCKER

There is risk you cannot afford to take [and] there is risk you cannot afford not to take.

— PETER DRUCKER

Only those who will risk going too far can possibly find out how far one can go.

— T. S. ELIOT

Risk varies inversely with knowledge.

— IRVING FISHER

The people I want to hear about are the people who take risks.

— ROBERT FROST

Two roads diverged in a wood, and I—
    I took the one less traveled by,
And that has made all the difference.

— ROBERT FROST

One doesn't discover new lands without consenting to lose sight of the shore for a very long time. — ANDRÉ GIDE

If we are intended for great ends, we are called to great hazards. — JOHN HENRY

And the trouble is, if you don't risk anything, you risk even more. — ERICA JONG

Only those who dare to fail greatly can ever achieve greatly. — ROBERT F. KENNEDY

If the creator had a purpose in equipping us with a neck, he surely meant us to stick it out. — ARTHUR KOESTLER

To be alive at all involves some risk. — HAROLD MACMILLAN

Get fired. If you're not pushing hard enough to get fired, you're not pushing hard enough. — TOM PETERS

What is necessary is never a risk. — CARDINAL DE RETZ

Don't let the fear of striking out hold you back. — BABE RUTH

Be wary of the man who urges an action in which he himself incurs no risk. — JOAQUIN SETANTI

If you're never scared or embarrassed or hurt, it means you never take any chances. — JULIA SOREL

Venture all; see what fate brings. — VIETNAMESE PROVERB

Being on the tightrope is living; everything else is waiting.

— KARL WALLENDA

All life is the management of risk, not its elimination.

— WALTER WRISTON

See also Boldness; Courage; Fear

SELF-DISCIPLINE

Hold yourself responsible for a higher standard than anybody else expects of you. Never excuse yourself. Never pity yourself. Be a hard master to yourself—and be lenient to everybody else.

— HENRY WARD BEECHER

Many people lose their tempers merely from seeing you keep yours.

— FRANK MOORE COLBY

Avarice, envy, pride,
Three fatal sparks, have set the hearts of all
On Fire.

— DANTE

The most important thing is to learn to rule oneself.

— JOHANN WOLFGANG VON GOETHE

Nothing gives one person so much of an advantage over another as to remain unruffled in all circumstances.

— THOMAS JEFFERSON

It is with our passions as it is with fire and water; they are good servants, but bad masters.

— ROGER L'ESTRANGE

What we do upon some great occasion will probably depend on what we already are; and what we are will be the result of previous years of self-discipline. — H. P. Liddon

I confront tough problems without flapping. Actually, I have a reputation for being the coolest person in the room. I've trained myself to be that. — Richard M. Nixon

Keep cool and you command everybody.
— Louis Léon de Saint-Just

The happiness of a man in this life does not consist in the absence but in the mastery of his passions.
— Alfred, Lord Tennyson

See also Anger; Fear

SELF-RENEWAL

When you forget the beginner's awe, you start decaying.
— Nobuko Albery

I do not try to dance better than anyone else. I only try to dance better than myself. — Mikhail Baryshnikov

I cannot stress too much the need for self-invention. To be authentic is literally to be your own author . . . to discover your own native energies and desires, and then to find your own way of acting on them. — Warren Bennis

Effective leaders maintain a learning posture throughout their lifetimes. — J. Robert Clinton

Be careful to preserve your health. It is a trick of the devil, which he employs to deceive good souls, to incite them to do more than they are able, in order that they may no longer be able to do anything. — VINCENT DE PAUL

Successful careers are not planned. They develop when people are prepared for opportunities because they know their strengths, their method of work, and their values.

— PETER DRUCKER

A calm temperament expectant of good.
— CHARLES WILLIAM ELIOT (PRESIDENT OF HARVARD UNIVERSITY, AT AGE 88,
ACCOUNTING FOR HIS GOOD HEALTH AND STRONG MIND)

Learn to laugh; it is a discipline to be mastered. Let go of the everlasting burden of always needing to sound profound.
— RICHARD J. FOSTER

One ought, every day at least, to hear a little song, read a good poem, see a fine picture, and, if it were possible, to speak a few reasonable words. — JOHANN WOLFGANG VON GOETHE

To exercise leadership, one has to expect to get swept up in the music. One has to plan for it and develop scheduled opportunities that anticipate the need to regain perspective. Just as leadership demands a strategy of mobilizing people, it also requires a strategy of deploying and restoring one's own spiritual resources. — RONALD A. HEIFETZ

Work is not always required of a man. There is such a thing as sacred idleness, the cultivation of which is now fearfully neglected. — GEORGE MACDONALD

Men of good will saddled with the fate of others need great courage to be idle when only rest can clear their fuddled wits.

— LORD MORAN

Read every day something no one else is reading. Think every day something no one else is thinking. It is bad for the mind to be always a part of unanimity.

— CHRISTOPHER MORLEY

Because we do not rest, we lose our way. We miss the compass points that show us where to go. We lose the nourishment that gives us succor. We miss the quiet that gives us wisdom. Poisoned by the hypnotic belief that good things come only through tireless effort, we never truly rest. And for want of rest, our lives are in danger.

— WAYNE MULLER

After you've done a thing for two years, you should look at it carefully. After five years, look at it with suspicion. After ten years, throw it away and start all over.

— ALFRED E. PERLMAN

The greatest mistake a man can make is to sacrifice health for any other advantage.

— ARTHUR SCHOPENHAUER

Life is like a ten-speed bike. Most of us have gears we never use.

— CHARLES SCHULZ

There must be more to life than having everything.

— MAURICE SENDAK

Self-love, my liege, is not so vile a sin as self-neglecting.

— WILLIAM SHAKESPEARE, *Henry V*

Be absolutely determined to enjoy what you do.

— GERRY SIKORSKI

The trouble with the rat-race is that even if you win, you're still a rat. — LILY TOMLIN

People who cannot find time for recreation are obligated sooner or later to find time for illness. — JOHN WANAMAKER

We should all do what, in the long run, gives us joy, even if it is only picking grapes or sorting the laundry. — E. B. WHITE

See also Ambition—Promise and Pitfalls; Humility; Priorities

SERVANT LEADERSHIP

My mother, a Jewish immigrant from Lithuania, used to tell her seven kids, "All my children are excellent. What's the big deal? Go do some good in the world and I'll be impressed." — MORTON I. ABRAMOWITZ

Men in great place are thrice servants: servants of the sovereign or state, servants of fame, and servants of business. — FRANCIS BACON

Whoever wants to become great among you must be your servant, and whoever wants to be first must be your slave. — THE BIBLE, MATTHEW 20:26-27

Leadership is giving. Leadership is an ethic, a gift of oneself. It is easy to miss the depth and power of this message. . . . The essence of leadership is not giving things or even providing visions. It is offering oneself and one's spirit. — LEE G. BOLMAN AND TERRENCE E. DEAL

All service is the same with God.

— ROBERT BROWNING

The first responsibility of a leader is to define reality. The last is to say thank you. In between, the leader is a servant.

— MAX DEPREE

Service is the rent we each pay for living. It is not something to do in your spare time; it is the very purpose of life.

— MARIAN WRIGHT EDELMAN

The true measure of a man is not the number of servants he has, but the number of people he serves.

— ARNOLD H. GLASGOW

There are two kinds of leaders: there is the man or woman who creates the self—his/her life—out of the drive of personal ambition, and there is the man or woman who creates a self out of response to people's needs.　　　— NADINE GORDIMER

Every kind of service necessary to the public good becomes honorable by being necessary.　　　— NATHAN HALE

Your position never gives you the right to command. It only imposes on you the duty of so living your life that others can receive your orders without being humiliated.

— DAG HAMMARSKJÖLD

To command is to serve, nothing more and nothing less.

— ANDRÉ MALRAUX

True greatness, true leadership, is achieved not by reducing men to one's service but in giving oneself in selfless service to them.　　　— OSWALD SANDERS

I don't know what your destiny will be, but one thing I know, the only ones among you who will be really happy are those who have sought and found how to serve.

— ALBERT SCHWEITZER

The general who advances without coveting fame and retreats without fearing disgrace, whose only thought is to protect the country and do good service to his sovereign, is the jewel of the kingdom.

— SUN TZU

Joy can be real only if people look upon their life as a service, and have a definite object in life outside themselves and their personal happiness.

— LEO TOLSTOY

A wise leader remembers that people perceive service in their own terms.

— UNKNOWN

Leadership is a serving relationship that has the effect of facilitating human development.

— TED WARD

If you wish to be a leader you will be frustrated, for very few people wish to be led. If you aim to be a servant you will never be frustrated.

— FRANK F. WARREN

The princes among us are those who forget themselves and serve mankind.

— WOODROW WILSON

He who does not know how to serve cannot know how to command.

— YUGOSLAV PROVERB

See also Humility

SUCCESS

The toughest thing about success is that you've got to keep on being a success. — IRVING BERLIN

Don't confuse fame with success. One is Madonna; the other is Helen Keller. — ERMA BOMBECK

The greatest orator in the world is success.

— NAPOLEON BONAPARTE

There is an obvious cure for failure—and that is success. But what is the cure for success? — DANIEL J. BOORSTIN

Becoming number one is easier than remaining number one.

— BILL BRADLEY

To find his place and fill it is success for a man.

— PHILLIPS BROOKS

It takes twenty years to become an overnight success.

— EDDIE CANTOR

For every hundred persons able to deal with adversity, there's only one able to deal with success. — THOMAS CARLYLE

Success consists of going from failure to failure without loss of enthusiasm. — WINSTON CHURCHILL

If a man aspires to the highest place, it is no dishonor to him to halt at the second, or even at the third. — CICERO

There is plenty of room at the top, but no room to sit down.

— MARY CROWLEY

Everybody battles for success; too few people are aware of its profound impact. Success tends to breed arrogance, complacency and isolation. Success can close a mind faster than prejudice. Success is fragile, like a butterfly. We usually crush the life out of it in our efforts to possess it.   — Max DePree

The secret of success in life is for a man to be ready when his time comes.   — Benjamin Disraeli

The secret of success is constancy of purpose.

— Benjamin Disraeli

Success seems to be largely a matter of hanging on after others have let go.   — William Feather

There is no point at which you can say, "Well, I'm successful now. I might as well take a nap."   — Carrie Fisher

Our greatest glory consists not in never falling, but in rising every time we fall.   — Oliver Goldsmith

One of the paradoxes of success is that the things . . . which got you there, are seldom those that keep you there.

— Charles Handy

Pray that success will not come any faster than you are able to endure it.   — Elbert Hubbard

The exclusive worship of the bitch-goddess *Success* [is] our national disease.   — William James

You have to create a climate that suggests success is imminent.

— Charlene Mae Knight

Victory is not won in miles, but in inches. Win a little now, hold your ground, and later win a little more.

— LOUIS L'AMOUR

The worst that can happen to a man is to succeed before he is ready.
— MARTIN LLOYD-JONES

The real demon is success—the anxieties engendered by this quest are relentless, degrading, corroding. What is worse, there is no end to this escalation of desire.
— MARYA MANNES

Success often depends upon knowing how long it will take to succeed.
— MONTESQUIEU

There is only one success—to be able to spend your life in your own way.
— CHRISTOPHER MORLEY

Success often comes to those who dare and act; it seldom goes to the timid who are ever afraid of the consequences.

— JAWAHARLAL NEHRU

It is the old lesson—a worthy purpose, patient energy for its accomplishments, a resoluteness undaunted by difficulties, and then success.
— W. M. PUNSHON

I have no expectation of making a hit every time I come to bat.
— FRANKLIN D. ROOSEVELT

Success is doing what you do well and letting others do everything else.
— UNKNOWN

Success can make you go one of two ways. It can make you a prima donna, or it can smooth out the edges, take away the insecurities, let the nice things come out.
— BARBARA WALTERS

Success is to be measured not so much by the position that one has reached in life as by the obstacles which he has overcome while trying to succeed. — BOOKER T. WASHINGTON

The way to succeed is to double your failure rate.

— THOMAS J. WATSON JR.

See also Experience; Failure; Fame and Recognition

TALENT

Doing easily what others find difficult is talent; doing what is impossible is genius. — HENRI FREDERIC AMIEL

Natural ability without education has more often raised a man to glory and virtue than education without natural ability. — CICERO

Great talent takes time to ripen.

— GREEK PROVERB

There is something much more scarce, something rarer than ability. It is the ability to recognize ability. — ROBERT HALF

Perseverance is the most overrated of traits, if it is unaccompanied by talent; beating your head against a wall is more likely to produce a concussion in the head than a hole in the wall. — SYDNEY J. HARRIS

There is no substitute for talent. Industry and all the virtues are of no avail. — ALDOUS HUXLEY

Everyone has talent. What is rare is the courage to follow the talent to the dark place where it leads. — ERICA JONG

Talent is God-given; be thankful. Conceit is self-given; be careful. — THOMAS LA MANCE

Talent is always conscious of its own abundance, and does not object to sharing. ALEKSANDR SOLZHENITSYN

If you want a track team to win the high jump, you find one person who can jump seven feet, not seven people who can jump one foot. — FREDERICK E. TERMAN

Use what talents you possess: the woods would be very silent if no birds sang there except those that sang best.
— HENRY VAN DYKE

There is only one proof of ability: action.
— MARIE VON EBNER-ESCHENBACH

Men are often capable of greater things than they perform. They are sent into the world with bills of credit, and seldom draw to their full extent. — HORACE WALPOLE

See also People Skills

TECHNOLOGY

During my 87 years I have witnessed a whole succession of technological revolutions. But none of them has done away with the need for character in the individual or the ability to think. — BERNARD M. BARUCH

Any sufficiently advanced technology is indistinguishable from magic.
— ARTHUR C. CLARKE (ATTRIBUTED)

Understand the technology you work for so well that you control *it* instead of letting *it* control *you.*
— GEORGE W. DUDLEY

Modern man worships at the temple of science, but science tells him only what is possible, not what is right.
— MILTON S. EISENHOWER

Machinery is aggressive. The weaver becomes a web, the machinist a machine. If you do not use the tools, they use you.
— RALPH WALDO EMERSON

A computer will not make a good manager out of a bad manager. It makes a good manager better faster and a bad manager worse faster.
— EDWARD M. ESBER

The danger of the past was that men became slaves. The danger of the future is that men may become robots.
— ERICH FROMM

The drive toward complex technical achievement offers a clue to why the U.S. is good at space gadgetry and bad at slum problems.
— JOHN KENNETH GALBRAITH

If you put tomfoolery into a computer, nothing comes out but tomfoolery. But this tomfoolery, having passed through a very expensive machine, is somehow ennobled and no one dares criticize it.
— PIERRE GALLOIS

Once technology is out of the jar, you can't put it back in.
— ERVIN L. GLASPY

The real danger is not that computers will begin to think like men, but that men will begin to think like computers.

— SYDNEY J. HARRIS

One machine can do the work of fifty ordinary men. No machine can do the work of one extraordinary man.

— ELBERT HUBBARD

Technology brings us powerful tools and incredible capabilities. It also sets a brutal pace for us to follow. — DAVE IRVINE

Our scientific power has outrun our spiritual power. We have guided missiles and misguided men. — MARTIN LUTHER KING JR.

You cannot endow even the best machine with initiative. The jolliest steam-roller will not plant flowers. — WALTER LIPPMANN

No automatic system can be intelligently run by automatons —or by people who dare not assert human intuition, human autonomy, human purpose. — LEWIS MUMFORD

Computers are useless. They can only give you answers.

— PABLO PICASSO

There are three roads to ruin—women, gambling and technicians. The most pleasant is with women, the quickest is with gambling, but the surest is with technicians.

— GEORGES POMPIDOU

Technology feeds on itself. Technology makes more technology possible. — ALVIN TOFFLER

TIME AND TIME MANAGEMENT

Time is a dressmaker specializing in alterations.

— FAITH BALDWIN

Always do one thing less than you think you can do.

— BERNARD M. BARUCH

A first-rate organizer is never in a hurry. He is never late. He always keeps up his sleeve a margin for the unexpected.

— ARNOLD BENNETT

Don't say you don't have enough time. You have exactly the same number of hours per day that were given to Helen Keller, Pasteur, Michelangelo, Mother Teresa, Leonardo da Vinci, Thomas Jefferson and Albert Einstein.

— H. JACKSON BROWN JR.

We can outrun the wind and the storm, but we cannot outrun the demon of Hurry.   — JOHN BURROUGHS

You will never "find" time for anything. If you want time you must make it.   — CHARLES BUXTON

The goodness that thou mayest do this day, do it; and . . . delay it not till tomorrow.   — GEOFFREY CHAUCER

Know the true value of time; snatch, seize, and enjoy every moment of it. No idleness, no laziness, no procrastination; never put off till tomorrow what you can do today.

— LORD CHESTERFIELD

Time management is really a misnomer—the challenge is not to manage time, but to manage ourselves.   — STEPHEN R. COVEY

Unless a person takes charge of them, both work and free time are likely to be disappointing.   — MIHALY CSIKSZENTMIHALYI

Time goes, you say? Ah no!
  Alas, Time stays, we go.

— HENRY AUSTIN DOBSON

Everything requires time. It is the only truly universal condition. All work takes place in time and uses up time. Yet most people take for granted this unique, irreplaceable and necessary resource. Nothing else, perhaps, distinguishes effective executives as much as their tender loving care of time.

— PETER DRUCKER

Time is really the only capital that any human being has, and the only thing he can't afford to lose.   — THOMAS EDISON

We all find time to do what we really want to do.

— WILLIAM FEATHER

There is more to life than increasing its speed.

— MAHATMA GANDHI

Time is the least thing we have.

— ERNEST HEMINGWAY

If you want work well done, select a busy man; the other kind has no time.   — ELBERT HUBBARD

You get very little sympathy these days for not managing your own time and stress. A generation ago people would say, "Poor George, worked himself to death, good man." Now they say, "What a fool, couldn't keep himself in balance."

— JENNIFER JAMES

Hell, by the time a man scratches his ass, clears his throat, and tells me how smart he is, we've already wasted fifteen minutes.

— LYNDON B. JOHNSON

Do today's duty, fight today's temptation; do not weaken and distract yourself by looking forward to things you cannot see, and could not understand if you saw them.

— CHARLES KINGSLEY

I'm continually asking myself, "What is the best use of my time right now?"

— ALAN LAKEIN

Don't do anything someone else can do for you.

— BILL MARRIOTT

I must govern the clock, not be governed by it.

— GOLDA MEIR

Work expands so as to fill the time available for its completion.

— C. NORTHCOTE PARKINSON

We think much more about the use of our money, which is renewable, than we do about the use of our time, which is irreplaceable.

— STEPHAN RECHTSCHAFFEN

Control your own time. Don't let it be done for you. If you are working off the in-box that is fed to you, you are probably working on the priority of others.

— DONALD RUMSFELD

God never imposes a duty without giving time to do it.

— JOHN RUSKIN

Remember that it was God who decided on a 24-hour day, and he must have felt it was enough. We can never do all that we expect ourselves to do, and we can rarely do all that others expect us to do, but we can always do all that God expects us to do. — SCOTT SERNAU

Make use of time, let not advantage slip.

— WILLIAM SHAKESPEARE, *VENUS AND ADONIS*

Time is the deposit each one has in the bank of God and no one knows the balance. — RALPH SOCKMAN

For fast-acting relief, try slowing down.

— LILY TOMLIN

See also Priorities

VALUES AND BELIEFS

It is easier to fight for one's principles than to live up to them.

— ALFRED ADLER

A man's life does not consist in the abundance of his possessions. — THE BIBLE, LUKE 12:15

Extremism in the defense of liberty is no vice. . . . Moderation in the pursuit of justice is no virtue. — BARRY GOLDWATER

If you really live your beliefs and make them attractive, you won't have to ram them down other people's throats—they will steal them. — DICK GREGORY

Error of opinion may be tolerated where reason is left free to combat it.

— Thomas Jefferson

The heresy of one age becomes the orthodoxy of the next.

— Helen Keller

There are two ways to slide easily through life: to believe everything and to doubt everything. Both ways save thinking.

— Alfred Korzybski

Nothing is more conducive to peace of mind than not having any opinion at all.

— Georg Christoph Lichtenberg

The dogmas of the quiet past are inadequate to the stormy present.

— Abraham Lincoln

Toward no crimes have men showed themselves so cold-bloodedly cruel as in punishing differences in belief.

— James Russell Lowell

One person with a belief is equal to a force of ninety-nine who only have an interest.

— John Stuart Mill

Where it is a duty to worship the sun it is pretty sure to be a crime to examine the laws of heat.

— John Morley

Experience dulls the edges of all our dogmas.

— Gilbert Murray

The most savage controversies are those about matters as to which there is no good evidence either way.

— Bertrand Russell

Fanaticism consists of redoubling your efforts when you have forgotten your aim. — GEORGE SANTAYANA

A thing is not necessarily true because a man dies for it.
— OSCAR WILDE

Every dogma has its day, but ideals are eternal.
— ISRAEL ZANGWILL

See also Clear Thinking; Open-mindedness

VISION

A vision is a target that beckons. . . . [A] vision always refers to a *future* state, a condition that does not presently exist and never existed before. With a vision, the leader provides the all-important bridge from the present to the future of the organization. — WARREN BENNIS AND BURT NANUS

In the absence of a vision, personality will prevail.
— DAN BOFFEY

A leader is one who sees more than others see, who sees farther than others see, and who sees before others do.
— LEROY EIMS

The most successful leader of all is one who sees another picture not yet actualized. He sees the things which belong in his present picture but which are not yet there. . . . Above all, he should make his co-workers see that it is not *his* purpose which is to be achieved, but a common purpose, born of the desires and the activities of the group. — MARY PARKER FOLLETT

The essence of leadership is a vision you articulate clearly and forcefully on every occasion. You can't blow an uncertain trumpet.
— Theodore Hesburgh

The vision of things to be done may come a long time before the way of doing them becomes clear, but woe to him who distrusts the vision.
— Jenkin Lloyd Jones

Take from the altar of the past the fire, not the ashes!
— Jean Jures

The most pathetic person in the world is someone who has sight but has no vision.
— Helen Keller

Men will not live without vision; that moral we do well to carry away with us from contemplating, in so many strange forms, the record of the visionaries. If we are content with the humdrum, the second-best, the hand-over-hand, it will not be forgiven us.
— Ronald Knox

A leader ought to be an incredibly competent, reliable person who follows through and is organized. But more than that, a leader has to have vision. Vision makes a true leader.
— Wendy S. Kopp

Leadership defines what the future should look like, aligns people with that vision, and inspires them to make it happen despite the obstacles.
— John Kotter

All men dream; but not equally. Those who dream by night in the dusty recesses of their minds wake to find that it was vanity; but the dreamers of the day are dangerous men, for they may act their dreams with open eyes, to make it possible.
— T. E. Lawrence

There is no more powerful engine driving an organization toward excellence and long-range success than an attractive, worthwhile, achievable vision for the future, widely shared.

— BURT NANUS

Think big. It's wonderful when it comes off.

— SIMEON NKOANE

Inspiring visions rarely (I'm tempted to say never) include numbers.

— TOM PETERS

The great leader can employ a talented person to handle administrative details. But it is impossible to hire a vision.

— WES PIPPERT

Visionary people are visionary partly because of the very great many things they don't see.

— BERKELEY RICE

To be a good leader you have to have a clear vision of what you want to get done, and keep focused on that vision. The problem in this society is that there is so much going on. The only way you can lead is if you have a very short agenda.

— DONNA E. SHALALA

We have too many efficient technocrats and too few far-sighted visionaries.

— WILLIAM E. SIMON

Every age needs men who will redeem the time by living with a vision of things that are to be.

— ADLAI STEVENSON

Vision is the art of seeing the invisible.

— JONATHAN SWIFT

A task without vision is drudgery. A vision without a task is a dream. A task with vision is hope. — UNKNOWN

See also The Future

WISDOM

Wise men learn by other men's mistakes, fools by their own.
— H. G. BOHN

I do not believe in the collective wisdom of individual ignorance. — THOMAS CARLYLE

To retire is not to flee, and there is no wisdom in waiting when danger outweighs hope, and it is the part of wise men to preserve themselves for tomorrow and not risk all in one day. — MIGUEL DE CERVANTES

Be wiser than other people if you can; but do not tell them so. — LORD CHESTERFIELD

Common sense in an uncommon degree is what the world calls wisdom. — SAMUEL TAYLOR COLERIDGE

By three methods we may learn wisdom: First, by reflection, which is noblest; second, by imitation, which is easiest; and third, by experience, which is the bitterest. — CONFUCIUS

Wisdom consists of the anticipation of consequences.
— NORMAN COUSINS

All human wisdom is summed up in two words—wait and hope. — ALEXANDRE DUMAS

Where is the wisdom we have lost in knowledge? Where is the knowledge we have lost in information? — T. S. ELIOT

Solomon made a book of proverbs, but a book of proverbs never made a Solomon. — ENGLISH PROVERB

Wise men change their minds, fools never.
— ENGLISH PROVERB

The wise man draws more advantages from his enemies than the fool from his friends. — BENJAMIN FRANKLIN

In seeking wisdom, the first step is silence, the second listening, the third remembering, the fourth practicing, the fifth— teaching others. — IBN GABIROL

It is unwise to be too sure of one's own wisdom. It is healthy to be reminded that the strongest might weaken and the wisest might err. — MAHATMA GANDHI

Wisdom is the sunlight of the soul.
— GERMAN PROVERB

Knowledge can be communicated but not wisdom.
— HERMAN HESSE

Every man is a damn fool for at least five minutes every day; wisdom consists in not exceeding the limit. — ELBERT HUBBARD

The wise man is he who knows the relative value of things.
— WILLIAM INGE

Wisdom is learning what to overlook.
— WILLIAM JAMES

Honesty is the first chapter of the book of wisdom.

— THOMAS JEFFERSON

Wisdom and truth come to a man who truly says, "I am ignorant, I do not know."

— J. KRISHNAMURTI

One's first step in wisdom is to question everything—and one's last is to come to terms with everything.

— GEORG CHRISTOPH LICHTENBERG

One who is not wise himself cannot be well advised.

— MACHIAVELLI

What is strength without a double share of wisdom?

— JOHN MILTON

It is not wise to be wiser than is necessary.

— PHILLIPPE QUINAULT

Nine-tenths of wisdom consists of being wise in time.

— THEODORE ROOSEVELT

In seeking wisdom, thou art wise; in imagining that thou hast attained it, thou art a fool.

— BEN SIRA (ATTRIBUTED)

The beginning of wisdom is the definition of terms.

— SOCRATES

Wisdom is the right use of knowledge. To know is not to be wise. Many men know a great deal, and are all the greater fools for it. There is no fool so great a fool as a knowing fool. But to know how to use knowledge is to have wisdom.

— CHARLES HADDON SPURGEON

Seven characteristics distinguish the wise: he does not speak in the presence of one wiser than himself, does not interrupt, is not hasty to answer, asks and answers the point, talks about first things first and about last things last, admits when he does not know, and acknowledges the truth.   — THE TALMUD

It is characteristic of wisdom not to do desperate things.

— HENRY DAVID THOREAU

There can be no wisdom disjoined from goodness.

— RICHARD C. TRENCH

Wisdom is merely knowing what to do next.

— UNKNOWN

To acquire knowledge, one must study; but to acquire wisdom, one must observe.   — MARILYN VOS SAVANT

Not to know is bad, but not to wish to know is worse.

— WEST AFRICAN PROVERB

True wisdom consists in knowing one's duty exactly, true piety in acting what one knows. To aim at more than this is to run into endless mistakes.   — THOMAS WILSON

When a man is on the point of drowning, all he cares for is his life. But as soon as he gets ashore, he asks: "Where is my umbrella?" Wisdom, in life, consists in not asking for the umbrella.   — JOHN WU

See also Judgment

AUTHOR INDEX

ABOUT THE AUTHOR

GORDON S. JACKSON is the associate dean for academic affairs at Whitworth College in Spokane, Washington, and has taught journalism there since 1983. Gordon grew up in South Africa where he worked as a journalist for a news magazine. He received his undergraduate education in South Africa before obtaining a doctorate in mass communications at Indiana University. Gordon has written five books, including *Quotes for the Journey, Wisdom for the Way* (NavPress).